ANIMALS AS GODS

SHAPESHIFTING THROUGH ANIMISTIC AND TOTEMISTIC WITCHCRAFT

LADY WOLF

GREEN MAGIC

Green Magic
53 Brooks Road
Street
Somerset
BA16 0PP
England
www.greenmagicpublishing.com

Designed and typeset by K.DESIGN
Winscombe, Somerset

ISBN 9781916014060

GREEN MAGIC

CONTENTS

Dedication. 4

Introduction. 5

GETTING STARTED   13

    Chapter One: What is Shapeshifting 14

    Chapter Two: Exploration Through Observation 20

    Chapter Three: Activation Through Visualization 28

    Chapter Four: Connection and Meditation 32

    Chapter Five: Movement and Mirror Work. 36

    Chapter Six: Activation Through Ritual and Spell Work. 41

CELTIC ANIMALS AS GODS   49

    Chapter Seven: Raven 50

    Chapter Eight: Horse 62

    Chapter Nine: Deer. 71

    Chapter Ten: Swan 79

NORDIC ANIMALS AS GODS   91

    Chapter Eleven: Bee. 92

    Chapter Twelve: Hawk 106

    Chapter Thirteen: Wolf. 119

EGYPTIAN ANIMALS AS GODS   135

    Chapter Fourteen: Cow. 136

    Chapter Fifteen: Lion. 147

    Chapter Sixteen: Scorpion. 157

    Chapter Seventeen: Cobra 167

NATIVE AMERICAN ANIMALS AS GODS   181

    Chapter Eighteen: Grandmother Spider. 182

    Chapter Nineteen: Coyote 195

This book is dedicated to my Granddaughter Mijah who reminds me, every day, to see the magick in everything.

Thank you to my children Shelby, Gavriel and Asher and my Lover and best friend Mason of 20 years.

My gratitude and heartfelt appreciation to all the animals who have come into my life and left a void unfillable, "Duchess, Deacon, Twink, Tilly, Dandy, Sophie, Brutus, Toby, Dozer, Cayenne, Pepper, Whisper, Shadow, Duchess #2, Gizmo, Chamomile, Hop, Little John, Lucky, Rusty and Ginger."

And to the ones that bless my home now "Gus, Chewie, Odin, Freya, Lugh, Padfoot, Ripley, Sassy, Old Timer, Schneebly." Also, a big thanks to all the chickens, roosters, bunnies and goats that have inhabited our little homestead and gifted us eggs and milk, etc. I am so honored to have been able to share time and energy with you all, my furry, scaled, feathered friends who I call family.

INTRODUCTION

What if, as a society, we have been believing and living all wrong? What if the gods have been walking amongst us all this time?

The Ancient Ones, our dearly departed ancestors, were on to something. They looked to what was right in front of them for guidance, example and the way to truly live a life of balance. They didn't pray to some superior being in the sky or the heavens. Their gods actually sustained them with life providing sustenance; shelter, clothing and food. All of which are vital to survival!

Have you ever wondered why the beings of old, the ones we have through the ages called gods/goddesses always appear in both animal and human form? Why did the Ancient Ones name their clans and tribes after animals?

This concept of seeing "God" in all things has been lost, ignored and quite frankly practically eradicated. Humans are consuming at a rapid rate! Our planet which has been revered, honored and worshipped as a goddess, Earth Mother, Mother Gaia, Mother Nature by the very first civilizations, clans, tribes and agricultural people is being destroyed each second, of each minute, every hour and every day by the descendants of those primitive people who, in comparison, in many ways were not so primitive but far more advanced than we are today.

The domestication of animals began not long after the early agricultural people embraced farming and began to set up permanent settlements about 10–12,000 years ago. About two thousand years before that, the first domesticated plants were being embraced by the early civilizations from Mesopotamia, Africa, Eastern Asia and North and South America.

We know that plants were used not only for food, but also for shelter and clothing. Animals were being tamed, bred and used for meat, milk and their hides. Some experts believe that goats were the first to be domesticated, followed by sheep and chickens. Other experts believe the domestication of animals began with the grey wolf somewhere between 33,000–15,000 years ago.

Domestication of animals has evolved into three main categories of companionship, sources of food and working animals; with the definition of domestication being *"animals that have been selectively bred and genetically adapted over generations to live alongside humans."*

In today's society, the numbers of animals being bred for these three categories is astounding and would make anyone embrace veganism and consider joining in PETA's quest to end the inhumane killing of innocent creatures. But that is not the intent of this book. Rather, this book is designed to help modern day civilizations get back to a way of living in balance, harmony and deep adoration of seeing the animals as gods once again.

Maybe this shift in our conscious awareness will create a worldwide shift of how we as individuals, communities and civilizations can begin to do our part to heal the damage we have done to our beloved planet. Maybe, just maybe, we can make it possible for the future generation to find balance amongst ownership, domestication and maybe they can have a better outlook and relationship with animals as the ultimate messenger, guide, teacher and mentor. If we can turn back and begin to see the animals as gods, maybe we can stop killing them for our own gain. Maybe?

Let's for just a minute step away from that and ask what or who is God? The dictionary gives multiple definitions:

1. In Christianity and monotheistic religions, God is the creator and ruler of the Universe and source of all moral authority: the supreme being.
2. In other religions God is a superhuman being or spirit worshiped as having power over nature or human fortunes.
3. An adored, admired or influential person.

The worship of animals as godlike beings or deities appearing in animal form is a theriomorphic belief and most commonly known as being practiced by the Egyptians. However, we can see this phenomenon present in many religions such as Hinduism, Buddhism, and even Christianity.

This way of living was not so much "animal worship", rather the sacred power, essence and attribute of the revered deity(ies) was believed to be manifested in a particular animal that was thought to represent as an incarnation of that specific deity. This practice and way of living stems from the early people and civilizations having a deep and profound, oftentimes religious and ceremonial behavior towards animals when it came to the hunting and gathering. So, it begs one to ask if the early civilizations actually worshiped animals or, did they honor them as a vital tool necessary for their very survival, so the act of hunting, gathering and consuming became a religious ceremony?

By definition, *"animal worship refers to rituals involving animals, such as the glorifications of animal deities or animal sacrifice. When a god is respected or worshipped by means of representative animal, an animal cult is formed."* This belief and practice of animal worship has been considered a religion since the early 1800's. However, the goal of this book is not to make the practice of shapeshifting a religious experience, but rather to see that since the beginning there have been many civilizations and religions that include zoolatry into their rituals, traditions and ways of paying homage to the gods.

The purpose of this book is to adopt shapeshifting and zoolatry practices into everyday life and solitary practices to help the individual remember that animals have been revered as sentient divine beings since the beginning. By embracing shapeshifting, one can enter a more balanced and harmonious way of living.

As author, I am no expert. I am simply a constant student of life and, with almost two decades devoted to the path of a Shapeshifting Priestess, I decided to put my teachings and passion into writing in the hopes that this present world that has embraced domination and control over not just the animals but Nature herself, can wake up and remember that our ancestors, even though ancient and primitive, were onto something. It is my hopes that my granddaughter can grow up in this world and learn live as one with Nature and see the animals as the greatest teachers, messengers, mirrors, guides and mentors.

It's the first week of January and instead of the temperature outside being freezing, it's a warm sunny 34 degrees. I woke up not feeling the best and my normal Tuesday schedule was already tampered with due to a cancellation and I suddenly found myself home with nothing really to do.

Our bathhouse door faces south and there is so much heat coming through the glass window on the door that I decide to go outside and soak up some much-needed sunshine. Once I step outside, my skin immediately begins to absorb the heat. There is a rug on the ground that is dry from the sunshine and underneath where the dirt lies it is spongy, probably from all the snow that has accumulated and now melted. There are two fairly large log stumps next to the rug which make the perfect seat for an afternoon sun bath.

We live in a very remote area of Southern Utah with neighbors well over an acre away. Our road is dirt with no street lamps. During the afternoon it's a rare occasion to have any cars drive by. I strip completely bare, place a towel on the rug, close my eyes and begin trance breathing. The heat from the sun feels amazing and my mind begins to go on a journey. I'm seconds from "dropping in" to a deep meditative flow, when a loud flapping of what I know to be raven wings soars above me. The beating of wings sounding so close that I expect to find the raven, that I feed twice a day, perched before me on one of the log stumps. When my eyes briefly open I catch just a glimpse of shiny black wings swooping above me. Knowing that I had already left food out for the Raven I close my eyes, take a long breath and begin again right where I left off.

I am standing in the forest; there are clearings on both sides and tall trees that look like evergreens. In front of me in my mind's eye, in my meditation are the two large tree stumps and on one of them stands a very large white and brown timber wolf. I am very familiar with this particular wolf energy as I call upon wolf quite frequently. This time wolf just stands on all fours, waiting for me to do something. It's time. It's time to wake up energetically, spiritually and shake off the winter slump I have been in.

Focusing on wolf, wolf focusing on me, I begin to breathe differently, allowing myself connection. It's not long before, in my mind's eye, I look down and I am the wolf standing on the two large tree stumps. I flex my paws, digging the tips of the claws into the somewhat still damp wood of the stumps.

My breath exhales out warm. My sense of smell activated and I want to move. My body morphed into wolf begins to stretch. It's not long before I am off the tree stumps and running. Fast! My legs, all four, pushing into the ground of the forest floor, dirt clods ripped up from my paws and flinging through the air as I run as fast as I can.

If it is windy outside in the forest I cannot tell, but my fur is pushed back from the speed of my sprint. Suddenly the scenery changes and I am moving up a rocky hill, my stance changes, my claws dig in deeper, chunks of rock falling as I swiftly move in a zig-zag pattern up the hill that gets steeper and steeper. My breathing fast, my mouth hanging open, my tongue beginning to hang out to one side, inside I feel excitement, a sense of fulfillment. I consciously focus on letting go, leaving everything behind me with each swift pounce of my paws. I release. I release. I release. When I reach the top of the hill, I am invigorated! Alive. I sit and bring my focus back to my breath, taking an inhale to the count of four and exhale to the count of four. By my second breath, I am of human form once more sitting on the rug outside my bathhouse. I am aware of my surroundings and open my eyes to see the two large tree stumps before me empty, no wolf. My entire body inside and out feels alive, lighter and filled with an overwhelming sense of accomplishment. I feel awake!

What is shapeshifting? Websters dictionary will give the definition as "one that seems able to change form or identity at will. *Especially*: a mythical figure that can assume different forms (as of animals)."

I certainly do not think that I am "mythical". However, during my meditation or trance working I felt every bit a wolf. From the way my body moved, breathed and even smelled. I could feel the tiny hairs moving as I was running. I could smell intensely the forest, dirt and musky scent of other animals. I could hear and see as my claws scraped on the rocks as I was climbing up the hill gripping with all fours. But, "mythical?" No.

To be perfectly honest I can't remember when my journey with animal magick began. It could be my aging memory or the basic fact that I have always been surrounded by animals and viewed them as much more than just pets. My very first memory is with an animal.

My childhood was blessed with animals in the home, whether it was a dog, cat, bird or turtles. You could say that I have been working with animals as my personal guides my entire life. My earliest memory is with a dog. My sister's dog in fact her name was "Duchess." She was a black and white springer spaniel who had my shoe in her mouth. I vividly remember that I was wearing a pale pink 80's velor sweat suit and my shoes were pink. I was about two years old and really did not like that the dog had my shoe! My entire childhood was filled with pets. We always had pets in the home. From dogs, to cockatiels that my mother hand fed, to box turtles, animals were not just pets, they were family members. To this day my home is filled with animals and I am very grateful to my mother for encouraging a deep love and appreciation for animals as sentient, divine beings.

Looking back, I can see the pattern of distinct animals coming to me consistently over long periods of time. When I sat down and did the math, each animal that I felt an intense connection with stayed with me for about seven years, then a switch or shift would occur and a new animal would appear. The very first for me was turtles. I had a very fond appreciation of turtles and wanted one as a pet. I was about ten years old when my sister was working in the mall in a clothing store and a box turtle appeared. She made every attempt to locate where this turtle had come from but was unable to find the actual owner and brought it home to me knowing that I had always wanted a turtle. This was for me the beginning of a lifelong journey into shapeshifting and working with animals as totems. This first official pet for me was named "Maurice" after the clothing store "Maurices" where she was found. In the next seven years I would acquire more turtles.

At seventeen I was working at our local pet store. I was determined to be a veterinarian and devote my life to helping animals. I loved my job at the pet store. Due to my experience with raising turtles, I soon became the box turtle rehabilitation specialist. When a sick turtle would be brought in I would take it home and care for it. Turtles fascinated me and they still do. In fact, as I type

I see one of the three box turtles that I currently, house walking around my front room, most likely looking for food on the ground. I am now 40 so I have been working with turtles for 30 years!

There was always an animal. I think I spent more time with them than I ever did with friends. My animal friends seemed to understand me and appreciate me. As a teenager my "pets" were my counselors, listening to my worries and comforting me with slobbery kisses and soft cuddles. Now as an adult with kids of my own almost fully grown and a grand baby I see my animals differently. I see how my little granddaughter looks at them, trusts them and is learning from them and now more than ever I feel the call to share "shapeshifting" magick. I realize there are numerous books on animal totems, animal messengers and plenty of oracle books, websites, apps for your phone that will link you up to your "spirit animal" but I have felt inspired to put into writing a guide to shifting your subconscious state with that of an animal.

But as a teenager, there was a big shift coming and I was struggling as most teens do with finding my spark, that thing that defines me and makes me authentic. I was exploring many facets and pushing as many boundaries as I possibly could. A shift was in the making and while I loved turtles, I began to see butterflies everywhere! It could be that the movie with Paulie Shore "Son-in-law" had just come out and I was eager to get a butterfly tattoo just like the main character or it could have been that I was in need of spreading my wings and blossoming into a woman...Who knows? But, for the next seven years, butterflies were everywhere! Even when I began to date my now husband, our courtship, which was poetically short, was blessed with tiger swallowtails every day...Every day! Looking to animals as messengers and guides I took this daily sighting as an omen of fortune and I just knew this was my person and we would have a beautiful life together.

I fondly remember wearing a purple hippie dress and he and I were standing outside of a restaurant and a tiger swallowtail almost landed on me, it flew around us in the most joyful way. Kissed by magic! That was what I felt with the butterflies. Even on our wedding day we were gifted with butterflies.

At 24, after two kids and a third on the way and three moves, we were finally settled in our home in Cedar. I felt very unhappy and the opposite of butterfly energy. I was sinking into depression and, while I was engrossed in my natural herbalist schooling, I was just not feeling a connection to butterflies. I was in a searching mode. I remember feeling out of sorts, lost and I couldn't sleep.

We were still adjusting to our new home and community. I had met a local midwife who helped me through a very traumatic miscarriage and with a new pregnancy she was working with me as an apprentice. But I felt like direction in a spiritual manner was lacking. So being awake in the middle of the night laying there with my eyes open, I heard an owl hooting right outside our bedroom window.

For the next seven years owl was my primary messenger or primary totem. I dove into education. I questioned everything and looked to owls as guides to see things deeper and really explore. I officially left the religion of my childhood, embraced the learning and training I was receiving by the Master Herbalist and midwife I was fortunate to train with, and things in my psyche really began to open up exponentially. I relished the wisdom and insight of utilizing owl as my mentor.

Now at the age of 31, I anticipated a shift from owl towards something else! I wanted it so badly that I tried to force it. I did meditations to call in a new animal guide and nothing came through. I felt disconnected from owl and hungry for something more than just learning. I wanted to dive in and take action and I had no idea what animal I needed or would call upon to assist me with this new quest. One night I lay in my bed frustrated because I had just gone through another guided meditation to help me connect with animal totem energy and now I lay defeated. Then I suddenly felt hot breath on my face and saw clear as day a very large timber wolf staring right at me. Now of course, in Utah we do not have wolves and there was no possible way a wolf was going to be standing in front of me in my bedroom. But there she was! No denying it! I could smell her breath and feel the heat. Wolf coming through was a big shock! All the other animals I had a fondness of, I considered them my favorite animals. But wolves? No, they scared the living shit out of me! I quickly closed my eyes and attempted to think of a different animal but the wolf would not leave.

Out of all the animals that have come to me as messenger, each of them poignantly inspiring, it has been wolf that has pushed me, challenged me and helped me to step into and own my full self. An animal that, quite frankly, I was frightened to look at. Here I am at the age of 40 and wolf has broken the seven year cycle. I feel that there is still more for me to learn but I also feel that holding onto one particular animal as an anchor is no longer necessary. Which is why, while wolf may still be with me, I am able to progress through the practice of shapeshifting and call upon any animal with any need that I may have. Why? Well, to answer with a question. . .Why not? Animals are and always have been, from the beginning of time, teachers. Who showed the first people what was safe to eat? I believe it was animals.

I believe and will continue to believe that animals teach and speak to those who will listen.

This book is a guide, an exploration into what shapeshifting was, is and how it can be utilized in our modern world and solitary practices. This book will offer you tips and techniques to assist you. It is my hope that it will add to your personal solitary practice and way of life. Within these pages you will find ancient myths and legends. Most you are probably familiar with but may need to see how animals have been guiding gods and goddesses, or how gods and goddesses were guiding people, through animals. Also included are rituals, meditation, physical ways to embody particular animals through yoga, and tips on how to channel, morph and call upon particular animal energies to create balance, harmony and a more primal instinctual approach to your every day.

This book is intended to be a guide into the world of animism through totemism and shapeshifting. While there is no actual historical documentations that express the proper way to utilize these ancient belief systems, there are plenty of modern day devotional skills that will help each reader settle in and become more comfortable in creating a working relationship with each particular animal discussed in each chapter.

In advance, let me express my deepest gratitude, for this is a journey that has been floating within me for years, just waiting to be put into written words. It is time!

Getting Started

CHAPTER ONE

WHAT IS SHAPESHIFTING?

With every journey comes some prepping and planning. A first step. With our journey into the world and practice of shapeshifting, some key definitions are just that, a first step. By developing a basic understanding of the basis of the words we use in embracing a new technique, we can gain a more advanced perception in the hopes of implementing each technique in a more fluid and cohesive manner.

The encyclopedia defines **shapeshifting** as, "In mythology, folklore and speculative fiction, shapeshifting is the ability to physically transform through an inherently superhuman ability, divine intervention, demonic manipulations, sorcery, or having inherited the ability. The idea of shapeshifting is in the oldest forms of totemism and shamanism."

The dictionary defines shapeshifting as, "One that seems able to change form. A mythical figure that can assume different forms of different animals."

Totemism is belief in the kinship of a group of people with a common totem. The word totem is derived from the Ojibwe (Chippewa) word 'odoodem', meaning "his kinship group", signifying a blood relationship. Totemism was the practice of having a natural object or animate being, such as as a bird or animal, as the emblem of a family, clan or tribe. Totemism encompassed a system of tribal organization according to totems. A totem was believed to be mystically related to the group and therefore not to be hunted. Totemism is approximately a 50,000 year old system of belief in spirit-filled life and/or afterlife that can be attached to or be expressed in things or objects. **Totem –** an object such as an animal or plant that serves as an emblem of a family or clan. Revered and honored symbol.

Totem poles were not worshipped within the belief of totemism. Their primary purposes were to commemorate specific people and events that were associated with the lineage of the particular tribes.

Damein Marie Thorpe, an atheist and humanist who is also an advocate and activist and very knowledgable on animism, totemism and much much more, states that, "*Totemism is a religion that uses nature as a model for society. Totems can be animals, plants or geographic features. People relate to nature through their totemic association with natural species. Totems are sacred emblems symbolizing common identity.*"

While most are familiar with the terminology of animal totems and the practice of totemism stemming from the North American tribes please keep in mind that our country of America is relatively young and the practice of totemism did not appear in America, nor was it only practiced in America. The practice of totemism actually stems from the early clans of Britain. Let me be perfectly clear I am not of Native American descent, so my focus and practice stems from the early Celts.

Although totems are often the focus of ritual behavior, it is generally agreed that totemism is not a religion. Totemism can certainly include religious elements in varying degrees, just as it can appear conjoined with magic. Totemism is frequently mixed with different kinds of other beliefs, such as ancestor worship, ideas of the soul, or animism.

Animism – is a belief based on the spiritual idea that the Universe, and all natural objects within the Universe, have souls or spirits. It is believed that souls or spirits exist not only in humans but also in animals, plants, trees, rocks, etc. This belief system is approximately 100,000 years old. Although each culture has its own different mythologies and rituals, "animism" is said to describe the most common, foundational thread of indigenous peoples' "spiritual" or "supernatural" perspectives

Anthropomorphism – is the attribution of human traits, emotions, or intentions to non-human entities.

In Latin, "anima" means "breath" or "soul" and "animalis", the adjective that comes from it means "having breath or soul." The word animal is also derived from the word "anima" which in Greek simply means soul. When implementing shapeshifting through animism, we will be calling upon the spirit or essence of each animal as a way of embodying shared attributes. After all, we are animals too!

Now I am no shaman, nor am I a representative of any native tribe, clan or nationality. Rather, my roots and ancestors are of English, Irish and Scottish decent. I have, through my years of learning within the realms of dabbling in shapeshifting, shifted my dialogue from what I previously referred to as "animal totem connection" by my own ignorance and lack of actual knowledge; to that of the actual practice of shapeshifting through animism and some totemism through definition and techniques mingled with my own as a Wiccan High Priestess, Ritual Priestess, hypnotherapist and animal activist.

The techniques discussed within this book are ones that I have formulated through trial, error and time and energy invested into formulating my own Wiccan Tradition "Desert Sage Witchcraft" and I practice both as a solitary witch and as a Coven Priestess and community leader.

By no means am I implementing that my way is the only way or even actual way that the ancestors practiced, for I am not a direct spokesperson for them. I can only speak for myself and what has worked for me. My practice stems from 26 years of ups, downs, mishaps and incredible rituals within the realms of a practicing witch, to animal workings one on one through training with a local veterinarian in my youth, employee at our local pet store, reptile specialist, to my short and humble years of service as a sworn in Animal Control Officer for our local law enforcement. As a lover of animals, I have never NOT had an animal in my home. My house is technically not mine, but rather my animals who graciously allow me to live here. My 40 years on this planet has gifted me with quite the ensemble of animal teachers. From all of this I have put together this book. The animals featured in this book are ones that I have spent time and devotion to through observation, visualization, meditative connection and physical embodiment through yoga and mirror work.

The shapeshifting techniques you will learn throughout this book will help you the reader to tap into the concept of embracing, mirroring and activating particular animals and their attributes, strengths and unique characteristics to assist you in connecting with them on a deeper level in the hopes of obtaining balance and step into the role of student of Nature. Through these techniques, you will also gain a new perspective on ancient gods and deities that have been utilized, called upon and looked to as teachers and role models, but you will begin to see them as animals rather than supreme unobtainable supernatural beings. Overall, the basis and intention of this book is to help the individual awaken their own unique animal instincts. After all, we as humans are mammals and would benefit greatly from using our guttural instincts rather than ego.

Who practiced totemism? I think the better question is, who didn't practice totemism? Edward Burnett Tylor was a famous anthropologist who would identify totemism with early civilizations way of classifying their surroundings, rather than focusing on the ideal that it was merely a form of worshipping the plants and animals. While Scottish ethnographer John Ferguson McLennan would argue that all the early humans, pantheons and civilizations practiced some form of totemism and was known for his claim that the primitive cultures first religion was totemism. His belief was that totemism bound the clan together as a unit of society. McLennan's work was pioneering and inspired many more to study and dive into the depths of totemism, such as Sigmund Freud and James G. Frazer, who suggested that totems bind people together in social groups and served as an impetus for the development of civilizations.

https://www.firstthings.com/article/2019/08/woke-totemism

https://www.newworldencyclopedia.org/entry/John_Ferguson_McLennan

While we know that the word totem is derived from the Ojibwa word "ototeman" which translates to "one's brother-sister-kin," the same word, stated in 1791 by a British merchant, would translate to "a guardian spirit or an individual that appears in the form of an animal." The overall basis of both translations would be used to identify the separate clans with their own animal totems, creating a differential status of each clan or tribe. The totem names for each clan or tribe was selected from animals in their specific regions.

For decades, scientists and anthropologists would study where totemism stemmed from and why. They would spend years arguing and disputing, all adding their own truths as they saw them into their research. The basis of all the research done would agree upon the notion that honoring totems can be classified as a ritual or religious act, but the overall practice of totemism is not a set organized religion. The practice of adopting totemism through worship and rituals can be an individualist and intimate relationship of friendship or kinship between a specific animal or nature object and the person practicing.

Groups, clans and tribes still honor and recognize totemism within their history, such as the Aborigines, African Pygmies, early civilizations of Africa, Ugrians, West Siberians, India, Oceania, North and South America. The use of totems within groups was studied in depth by Emile Durkheim who wrote *The Elementary Forms of the Religious Life* which focused on the religious life of totemistic clans in the Aborigines. It should be noted that the Aboriginal culture is the oldest known culture.

The Aborigines call totemism "Kobong" and they have many clans named after totems, such as the Dingo and Water-Hen.

In his book, Durkheim states that all religions consist of collectively held and obligatory beliefs and practices organized around sacred objects. These objects embody a special energy. They are thought to be uniquely life-giving, which is why the rituals surrounding them are closely tied to sex, food, and the activities necessary to secure the survival of the clan. The Aboriginal religion is totemistic in the fact that their clan's totem is an actual physical entity of a plant or animal that the tribe(s) identify with. This totem is the primordial life-giving force that animates them, 'animate' in definition meaning: *to give spirit and support to.*

When we put totemism and animism together, the best way to separate both is to remember that totemism is linked to any species of plant or animal which is viewed, worshipped and honored as having supernatural powers. The belief and practice stems from the essence that the human gives the object. Animism is the belief that these species of plants and animals possess within them a spirit or source of energy not given by the person. Animism is the belief that ALL encompasses a life force, energy or spirit.

One could argue that animism predates Paganism as a belief system. Paganism is a religion other than one of the main world religions, specifically a non-Christian or pre-Christian religion, that incorporates beliefs or practices from outside the main world religions, especially nature worship.

The practice of totemism was more prevalent in the hunting and gathering civilizations. Animal worship and hunting rites have been proven through evidence found in cave art dating back to the Upper Paleolithic period of 40,000–10,000 years ago. These cave paintings are primarily depictions of animals which most scholars and scientists have agreed represent the primitive people's awareness and respect for animals as vital importance to their survival.

Shapeshifting is the physical act of incorporating totemism and animism practices into physical and tangible worship through visualization, body movement, meditation and ritual. "In mythology, folklore and speculative fiction, shapeshifting is the ability to physically transform through an inherently superhuman ability, divine intervention, demonic manipulations, sorcery, or having inherited the ability. The idea of shapeshifting is in the oldest forms of totemism and shamanism."

Shapeshifting was performed somewhat effortlessly by shaman, wise men, wise women and healers of tribes and clans. They seemed to have a gift for embracing their mental capacity and imagination allowing their souls to journey and blend with that of an animal. After all, the power of imagination is limitless. The power of our mind is limitless. If we are all connected through energy then naturally if we focused more intently and precisely, what couldn't we do? The ancient shaman knew this. Lauren Torres states, "shaman would say, that behind reality there is a web of life, that is a network of invisible linkages that interconnects things and people in inexplicable ways." She also goes on to say that "a shapeshift does not always have to involve something as radical as a human becoming a hawk. A shapeshifter can change their own energy slightly, for instance, to blend in to their environment."

Does one need to be a shaman or mystic healer to shapeshift? Absolutely not! The difference really is how the shaman, mystic healers and wise ones viewed their reality and understood their connection with the object, plant or animal they were shifting with. Is shapeshifting a primitive, indigenous, tribal, pagan, wiccan or witchcraft tradition? Not at all. In fact, there is an entire Christian community devoted to embracing animism. Dr. Graham Harvey, a Professor of Religious Studies says, "Animists are people who recognize that the world is full of persons, only some of which are human, and that life is always lived in relationship with others and all that exists lives. . .All that lives is holy."

When we disconnect from the religious ownership and go back to the source of all things being alive and filled with their own unique essence, energy and spirit, it is actually quite limitless who can embrace totemism and animism in not just their day to day, solitary or personal practice, but those that wish to enhance their religious experience can blend the practice of shapeshifting into their beliefs. After all, Jesus was known as the "lamb" of God for a reason.

ReWildUniversity has a lovely video you can watch on youtube which states that shapeshifting is a mental skill that anyone can develop. It increases your awareness, enjoyment of nature, hunting and foraging skills, ability to access instinctual survival skills in order to stay calm in stressful situations, and can overall increase one's mental fitness. This is done by tapping into one's imagination, a childlike imagination. Remember when you were little? As children, our imagination is alive and thrives in the worlds that we create. There is great power that occurs when we tap into that once again as adults.

https://youtu.be/VJK-QfoFeLk

It is also good to realize that shapeshifting is NOT limited to animals, but all things! The belief that all things, the tiniest pebble, plant, insect, tree, boulder and more, all possess their own energy and essence.

Another great quote is from Frank McKeown's book "The Mist-Filled Path", where he states, "The ancient shamanic art of shapeshifting is essentially the bioenergetic practice of attuning the rhythm of one's own shape to the rhythm of something in the natural world so that we may share its consciousness. . .This is not supernaturalism; rather, it is naturalism. . . Through the art of shapeshifting, and through various visionary and meditative techniques, we also begin to understand more fully the spiritual reality that everyone one of us has a reserved place within the great shape of things."

CHAPTER TWO

EXPLORATION THROUGH OBSERVATION

While knowing the basic definition is a great starting point or first step into any journey, taking time to observe is key. When it comes to animals, not everyone has a homestead like myself where one can sit and physically watch animals. We do, however, live in a world where technology has its perks. One of which is youtube. When I have a new student or client seeking to understand an animal that keeps coming through to them in dream work, meditation or even in the wild, the first thing I recommend is observation.

This Latin verb *observare* translates as *"to attend to"* and is the base word in 'observation', which means *"pay attention, take a patient look."* The key being 'patient look'. It is easy to glimpse at something and get a simple idea of what it is you are looking at, but to observe means to *"look"* at. By definition, *"the act of directing the eyes towards something and perceiving it visually."*

By taking the time and initiative to sit, watch and break down into fine details what one sees, you begin to absorb not only more knowledge of what you are observing but also a greater understanding. For example, when you plant a garden, crafting a planting journal is an excellent way of observing what each seed needs in order to germinate. What does each tiny plant need for survival and, upon harvest, how can you best preserve, store or consume each plant? The same can be implemented for your journey into shapeshifting.

If you were to simply say "I want to shapeshift with bear today without any observation," what would you gain? However, if you were to break it down and honor the steps of "observing" in a slow and patient manner, the attributes of bear would come into play. For example, what do bears eat, where do they live, how do they hunt, how are they hunted, how do they attack their prey and how are they attacked as prey, how do they find a mate, how do they mate, how do they care for their young, what parts of bear are consumed by their predators and what why? See how there are numerous things to be observed and digested before you call upon a particular animal.

The other thing to ask before you go into observation mode, is 'why'? Why are you wanting to embrace a deep connection and relationship with any particular animal? It is also a good idea to know oneself. After all, there are quite possibly traits that you possess that you do not want to amplify or bring to the surface. Just like there are some animals and their attributes that you may not want to embody and activate in your current life. Research and observation go hand in hand with setting the intention to connect with any particular individual animal species.

The other thing to remember is that intention is NOT everything! This is a common misinformed nuance that has been embraced by the modern day practitioner of witchcraft. Anyone can set an intention or intend to do something but without actual follow through and activation, there really is no intent being implemented. So, if you are going to take time to devote and shape shift with a particular individual animal, then why? How? What do you hope to gain? What do you intend to learn? There has to be follow through. When you are working with any animal in the facet of shapeshifting, you are doing so from a state of honor, respect and, for lack of better word, worship. So, take the time!

Observation tools are abundant. Youtube is quick and easy. One can literally sit down and type in "bear as prey" or "bear as predator" and a multitude of videos and links will pop up. There are also hundreds and thousands of documentaries that you would watch. There are also countless books one could read. However, I will caution on diving deep into books for insight on animal messages as, just like this book, the information you are reading is coming from the author's perspective and experience and, as with anything in life, it is vital to one's growth and expansion to formulate one's own opinion, perspective and relationship in place of an outside one. Again, I am no expert. I am simply a constant student of life and what works for me might not work for you, and that is okay!

Another key to observation is time. Move slow, be patient. Animals, like people, have good days and bad days. Expecting an animal to behave the same, day in and day out, is very unrealistic and a disservice to the animal you are observing. So, it is recommended that with your observation you take time, maybe days, weeks or even months learning about all the fine details of the particular animal you are intending to connect with. After all, you can meet someone face to face or through the virtual world that we live in and think you know them, but time is the only way of really knowing anyone or anything. With observation comes patience.

When I first began to offer workshops on animal totem activation, my focus was on helping the individual activate connection with their "primary totem" or main animal that is their mirror at the time and has been or will be for many years. Many years being up to seven, from my own personal experience. However, now I begin to see and understand that devoting oneself to a particular animal for that amount of time is the best way to fully understand and call upon animals as messengers. The more time you spend with any animal in a form of devotion, the more you learn, gain and understand. Feel free to devote yourself to a particular animal as long as you need. But know that other animals will still continue to appear when and if they have a message for you.

Also, it is imperative to know that shapeshifting is not limited to only animals. One can shift with any physical, tangible object found in nature. Have you ever participated in a meditation that suggested you reach down energetic roots and anchor into the earth? Or had strong legs like the trunk of a tree? I know I have, many, many times. In most ritual grounding meditations, there is a tree meditation. This kind of shift in our subconscious, to embrace the energy and essence of a tree, is a form of shapeshifting.

Keys to observation include, and are certainly not limited to, forming observation checklists. The first step is to select an object to observe. Will you begin with an animal or plant? Will the animal be wild or will you observe through virtual tools? Will the plant be one you currently have or will it be one you will venture out to discover and observe? See all the many variables and, more importantly, the opportunities.

MEDITATION EXERCISE #1

For this first exercise, I want you select an animal from your current surroundings. This can be a domesticated pet. Grab your journal and begin to move through the checklist below. Really take some time and observe all the fine details. More is better.

1. Physical characteristics
2. Behavioral characteristics
3. Eating patterns
4. Sleeping patterns
5. Interaction with surroundings
6. Expressive characteristics

With physical characteristics, really be detailed. Does the animal you are observing have scales, feathers or fur? What color is it? What color are its eyes?

How does it breathe? Through its mouth or nose? Is its breathing labored or steady? While you are observing, is the animal in a heightened state or a calm state? How is it reacting to you observing it? If there are other animals around, how is the particular animal you are observing interacting with them? What does this animal eat? How often? When does it sleep? Where does it sleep?

Once you have formulated your observation list, can you see any similarities between you and this animal? Since this is a domesticated animal, how can you embrace empathically? Empathy by definition is the ability to understand and share the feelings of others. Can you see the similarities if you put yourself in the position of a domesticated pet? So much of shapeshifting is observation and implementation of what is seen.

MEDITATION EXERCISE #2

For this next exercise, I want you to observe a plant in your home. Move through the checklist below and really take the time to see the fine details.

1. Physical characteristics
2. Species (edible or non edible?)
3. Unique properties (healing agent or decorative?)
4. Survival needs (water, soil, nutrients)
5. Plant history
6. Response to stimulus

Once your list is complete, spend some time with your plant on a day to day basis for a period of ten days. You may want to consider observing your plant at different times during the day. For example, if your plant is by a window, do its leaves turn to face the afternoon sun? When it comes to introducing stimuli there are many experiments that you can implement, but remember this is your plant and you are responsible for its health and well being.

One experiment I personally have done is with music, different types of music. Yes, some plants thrive on rock and roll and others seem to detest it. Some plants enjoy opera and some excel on meditative beats. Another experiment comes from giving your plant positive and negative feedback. In other words, yelling at your plant or talking to it with love and kindness will actually determine whether the plant thrives or begins to deteriorate. Again, this is your plant.

In your final observation, can you relate to this plant? Do you have any similarities with it? Refer back to your response to stimulus notes; when yelled at, do you thrive or dwindle? When spoken to with love and kindness, do you excel or retreat? While it is important to know and realize that one can shapeshift with any object, plant, insect or animal, for the purpose of this book the emphasis will be on shapeshifting with insects and animals as mirrors, messengers and guides.

By moving through these observation techniques, you can develop a greater understanding and relationship with the animal, plant or object that you are intending to shapeshift with. It is, after all, vital to have a basic knowing of what you intend to shapeshift with and why. For example, when it comes to shapeshifting with birds in the hopes of gaining a new perspective, you will want to be precise on what bird. Each bird has different attributes and qualities. For example, an owl sees best at night, whereas a hawk sees best during the day. An owl has binocular vision and a hawk does not. The key is to understand the attributes of the object, plant or animal in order to effectively tap into that energy and embody it within your own practice of shapeshifting. This is why observation is the first key.

Another key element in developing observation skills is to realize that ALL insects and animals (and that includes humans) are both predator and prey. Even the King of the Jungle is prey. Unfortunately, humans are his predators. Whether you are observing in person or through virtual means of youtube, documentaries or educational videos, allow yourself to see how each insect or animal being observed steps into prey mode and activates predator mode.

It is important to know that we are creatures of duality. Within us there are many opposites at work. For example, we both possess a feminine and masculine quality, light and dark, active and passive, motion and stillness. The active and passive could relate to predator and prey. When we look at the yin yang symbol of the Taoist religion, we see that this symbol represents this duality in nature and in all things. The following exercises with predator and prey are designed to shift one's perspective towards having empathy, which by definition is a feeling of awareness towards another's emotions and an attempt to understand how they feel. Empathy gives one the ability to not only understand but put yourself in the others shoes or paws and imagine what they are experiencing.

What if we began to be more aware of how our physical bodies reacted to a possible threat, discomfort or pleasure and actually trusted that guttural, instinctual feeling instead of arguing with it?

All too often in today's world humans have embraced the art of rationalization and weighing the pros and cons. We step into an ego driven mindset and forget that we are animals. Our body instinctively knows whether a situation or setting is going to be safe and in our best interests, or if we should just leave and return back to the safety of our den and pack. My goal with writing this book is to help you the reader gain that awareness and reclaim that instinct that we all have as animals. We can get back to living in a harmonious state of being one with Nature, as a part of Nature, not separate from her.

By taking time out the day and consciously focusing or setting personal intention to connect with an individual animal as teacher, mentor, guide or mirror; starting with observation is the key. Before you begin to embrace, for example, wolf energy, you should have a basic understanding of why wolves behave the way they do. Why and of what are they territorial? How and when do they act as prey, and to whom? What are their relationship cycles and behavior patterns like?

Whilst sitting down and observing wolf is not accessible to everyone, we do live in a virtual world where the internet has literally put just about everything in our hands with one swipe or click. Utilizing youtube or animal documentaries is a big help when it comes to observing animals in their habitat. One could, I suppose, go to a zoo and watch animals but these animals are not in their natural habitat but a human crafted impersonation of what their natural habitat may be.

When observing, I usually recommend that you have a journal and that you jot down notes.
For example, if you are watching a documentary on polar bears, it would be a good idea to jot down how these large animals hunt, gather and care for their young.

It's also important to really begin to see how each animal you work with has both a predator and a prey aspect. This is key in helping you on your journey with shapeshifting. When one can embrace prey aspects similar to how others embrace and work with their "shadow" self, one can really begin to experience the vulnerabilities that come with shapeshifting. It is not possible to shift with polar bear and not activate a polar bear's prey tendencies, nor is it advised. If we are working with animals to help enhance our solitary practices, relationships and more, then we need to allow both predator and prey essence to come through in our workings, otherwise we miss half of the practice.

When we apply observation as a valued tool, we can also begin to observe whichever deity we are working with that also displays those similar attributes to the particular animal we are calling upon. For example, when you work with Odin and his wolves or ravens, you also need to observe how Odin displayed prey characteristics, not just predator.

We are not that separate from the animal kingdom. In fact the similarities begin to appear in the most synchronistic of ways when we allow ourselves to fully observe animal and deity as whole unto themselves as prey and predators. This practice of seeing the whole animal, not broken or damaged like we see each other or ourselves, is one of the most profoundly altering effects of shapeshifting magick. When you can see yourself as whole unto self, just as we see animals through observation, we begin to activate that more primal side of ourselves and we break through the ego and fear-based patterns to step into living a fully conscious and present way of life.

MEDITATION EXERCISE #3

Give yourself some time at your computer for this research and observation exercise. Pick any animal or insect for example the black widow. Now type in black widow as prey and black widow as predator. You will have a large number of videos and articles pop up. Take some time to watch and observe whatever insect or animal you select as both predator and prey. Add these observations to your observation checklist. Once you have completed your research and lists take a good look. How and why did the object of your observation step into predator and step into prey? Can you relate in any way?

MEDITATION EXERCISE #4

For this exercise select a mammal, any mammal. Begin with exercise #1 and complete the observation checklist. Now go back to youtube and type in that mammal as both predator and prey. Write down your observations. For the acts of prey, can you observe what physically is happening and can you relate? For example, when you are perceiving an attack, how do you physically respond? Now go back to youtube and type in that mammal as predator. What are your observations? When it comes to shapeshifting with any animal, empathy is key. Through observation techniques like these you begin to see all the unique attributes and characteristics of the animal being observed and then, by looking to the animal as a mirror, you can begin to see the similarities you have or can relate to with that animal. While these techniques are not necessary to shapeshift they are certainly very helpful.

Caution
This exercise can create a physical reaction and can be uncomfortable to watch. For example, when I had my husband do this exercise, he picked his primary animal messenger, a bear. When he typed in bear as prey, unfortunately it was a video of a bear being shot by a human. Naturally, my husband was

very disturbed by this. Shouldn't we all be disturbed by this? In the video the bear was in its natural habitat and was exploring a nearby cabin when the owner's dog ran at the bear. Naturally, the bear was startled and on alert. Then when the owner rushed the bear the bear's natural defense mechanism upon feeling attacked was to charge, thus being shot and killed by the human. Just like a lion falls prey to humans, so do bears. It is equally disturbing to watch bear as predator to human and see how many bear attacks there are documented on film. The intent with this exercise is to hopefully present you the reader with a new perspective from the animal's point of view. Was the bear in the wrong to attack? Could it have had cubs nearby and been simply protecting its own? Was the human in the wrong? After all, the human could have had family that he was protecting?

CHAPTER THREE

ACTIVATION THROUGH VISUALIZATION

Once you have fully embraced the art of observation, it's time to focus on visualization. You tapped into this a bit through your observation lists by allowing yourself to "*see*" the similarities that you have with the object being observed. One technique of visualization is called 'exposure', which involves obtaining as much detail and information as possible on the subject or object that increases your knowledge and awareness, which is where your observation lists come into play. With your observation lists and techniques you enhance the possibilities and reasons as to why you are wanting to shapeshift with a particular animal. When I first began working with wolf, I was extremely hesitant and uncomfortable. Embracing a large predator that I did not know much about, other than what was projected in film, story books and others' experiences only added to my discomfort. However, once I set the intention and devotion, diving into video documentaries, factual books and having my own personal interaction with an actual wolf helped me to launch not just a connection but activation. Wolf and pack mentality has become the foundation of my priestess work, my witchcraft tradition and how I facilitate my coven. But that is for another book.

Before one can achieve any objective, goal or intent, one needs to first have a thought or visual idea of what that looks like. "We must see it to believe it." For one to shapeshift into anything really, you will need to be able to see it physically and then close your eyes and see it.

A social scientist, Frank Niles states, "According to research using brain imagery, visualization works because neurons in our brains, those electrically excitable cells that transmit information, interpret imagery as equivalent to a real-life action. When we visualize an act, the brain generates an impulse that tells our neurons to 'perform' the movement. This creates a new neural pathway -- clusters of cells in our brain that work together to create memories or learned behaviors -- that primes our body to act in a way consistent to what we imagined. All of this occurs without actually performing the physical activity, yet it achieves a similar result."

For the practice of shapeshifting, we will be combining *outcome* visualization with *process* visualization. Outcome visualization is defined as "creating within your mind the desired outcome using all your senses." After I had completed my training with hypnotherapy, I began taking hypnobirthing clients in my midwifery practice; one of the techniques that was taught to my clients was outcome visualization. I would have my clients visualize themselves in detail going through their labor experience in a calm and relaxed manner. Then I would have them visualize in detail their birth and create within their mind the desired outcome. Hypnobirthing has been proven to be very effective, largely in part to the way clients and their minds work together. For process visualization I would have my clients visualize everything they needed to do or the actions they needed to take in order to create their desired outcome or birth. For example, my clients would visualize themselves in the labor and birthing process as staying calm, focusing on their breathing techniques, being supported by their labor support and their nurses, doctors and so forth. By using both techniques together your thoughts begin to become your reality.

Emotional visualization is the next technique. To make the most of your shapeshifting experience, you combine the observation techniques with the visualization techniques with the last step being how does one feel when they focus on a particular goal, animal, object or intention? With my midwifery clients, their last visualization exercise was focused on seeing in detail the birth playing out, then allowing the client to feel the joy that comes with having a baby, the feeling of accomplishment and peace with the long wait being over and the baby being in your arms. When I worked with wolf, the emotions that I felt were strength within and the comfort of the security a pack provides.

Let us do a little exercise to show you how effective your mind is at perceiving and creating reality based off simply visualizing something that isn't right in front of you. As children our imagination is alive, wild and free. As adults, we have that same childlike capacity to imagine things, however, we have become busy. Our lists of responsibilities, bills, worries is different. As children we didn't have the heavy weight and often times burden that comes with being an adult. Our mind has simply become busy and very rarely do we take time to imagine, contemplate and meditate. The following is a very easy and brief visualization exercise that I learned in my hypnosis training.

MEDITATION EXERCISE #5

With your eyes closed, bring your focus to your breath. Taking a nice deep inhale followed with an exhale. Breathe in to the count of four and out to the count of four. Continue this breath pattern for four-eight breath cycles or until you feel your physical body moving into a relaxed state and your mind becomes calm and free of outside thoughts.

In your mind's eye picture yourself standing in your kitchen. See in detail the cabinets, countertops, appliances, flooring. Give yourself mental permission to really see yourself there in your kitchen. As you look around your kitchen, you notice something new a basket is sitting on the counter and it is filled with bright yellow lemons.

Allow yourself to see yourself walking over to the counter and picking up a lemon from the basket. See how bright and vibrant this lemon is, feel the wax-like texture of the lemon. Holding this lemon, you notice a cutting board and small, but effective knife. Place the lemon on the cutting board and, picking up the knife, you cut the lemon in half. Notice immediately how the juices of the lemon begin to pour out onto the cutting board. You can smell the fresh, citrus scent of the lemon.

Bring one half of the lemon up to your nose and really inhale that crisp, enlightening aroma. Now open your mouth and bite into this half of the lemon. Taste the lemon. Now open your eyes.

Some visualization follow up questions. Could you see your kitchen? Were you actually standing in your kitchen? Could you see the basket filled with lemons? Could you smell or taste the lemon?

Chances are you were able to see the kitchen, yourself there in the kitchen, the basket, lemon and you could smell the lemon. Most taste the lemon and cringe, while others simply have a physical reaction. For example, an increase in saliva or puckering of the face. The key to all of this is there was NO lemon. You, with the power of your mind, visualized it all. You did this based on *observations* and actual experiences with lemons. You have ample *exposure* to your kitchen daily, so picturing the details was not difficult. Then you combined both *outcome* and *process* visualization to create an *emotional* experience.

In my work I have had clients that do not like lemons that just the thought of biting into one makes their entire face cringe and they immediately open their eyes. Whether you could taste the lemon or not, your subconscious created a physical response.

This type of exercise can be applied to working with animals as messengers, guides or, for lack of a better word, totems. Throughout this book you will be exposed to a variety of animals. You will be given some basic background on each animal, myths, legends and even Deities associated with each animal. But it will be up to you to enhance your connection by developing your own observation lists. Anyone can pick up a book and read about an animal but, when it comes to shapeshifting, you the reader are the one that really implements the exercises shared and you are the one that enhances that connection by formulating your own relationship with each animal.

CHAPTER FOUR

CONNECTION THROUGH MEDITATION

Now that you have a basic understanding of what shapeshifting, animism and totemism are; along with some basic tips on developing observation keys to develop a fine understanding of the object, insect or animal, it is now time to focus on blending visualization with the power of meditation.

Meditation is a broad term with many different types of mediation, styles and techniques. The best way to find a meditation technique that works for you is through experience and trial and error. After all the only way to truly know if you feel the effects of something physically, mentally and spiritually is to take the time and experiment. I would say "try" but the word "try" is really not an action word. How can one ever actually "try" something? One either does it or doesn't. For example, one cannot "try" a piece of chocolate cake, you either take a bite or you don't.

By definition, 'meditate' means to engage in contemplation, reflection, to focus one's thoughts, to ponder. Meditation is the actual practice. This can be achieved through concentration, breath work, mantras and more. For this chapter we will go over some basic meditation techniques to help you take your practice of observation and visualization a bit deeper.

As an adult in our world of responsibilities and "to-do's" our subconscious mind and conscious mind are hardly ever lined up and in sync. We are busy and tend to go, go, go until right about when we lay down in bed, and then we become still. Some of us zone out or become still while reading a book or driving which is a symptom of the conscious and subconscious being lined up. The act of lining up the subconscious with the conscious is what makes meditation so effective. When we can line these parts of our brain up, we can absorb messages through our conscious surroundings. Such as guided words or prompts, and they become engrained into our subconscious.

For example, the lemon exercise. When you close your eyes and focus on your breath, you are allowing your conscious mind to rest so that your subconscious mind can be activated. Which is why visualizing the kitchen, lemons and encounter with the lemon scent and taste was so effective. Your subconscious chose those descriptions, messages and suggestions that you could see, smell and taste the lemon as your new reality. The mind is a powerful tool!

Meditation is a tool that trains your mind. Your mind is like a muscle; the more you work it the stronger it will become. So, the more you participate in meditation, the more responsive your mind is going to be to such messages that are sent through to the subconscious mind.

Throughout this book you have access to my personal style of guided meditation. There is no right or wrong way to meditate, the key is simply to take the time each day and do it. While my style is not for everyone, it is the style that I have found to be effective for myself and my clients. We begin with breath. The art of breathing in and breathing out. This is something that very rarely do we keep track of. It's a normal function of our body. By focusing on one's inhale and exhale in a conscious manner, one can step into a state of calmness where the mind is not wandering, worrying or creating distracting thoughts. By focusing on our breathing pattern, we enter a state of consciously being present. There is great magic in being present. Your inhale and exhale also help your physical body and mental body to relax. Have you ever noticed that it is almost impossible to have tension in your body when you exhale?

When I worked with women in labor as a doula I would have my clients focus on taking an inhale when their contraction would begin and their exhale would occur right about the peak of their contraction, allowing the laboring woman to relax during the contraction making the entire labor experience more effective. Let's practice.

MEDITATION EXERCISE #6

Take an inhale, breathe in to the count of four – one... two... three... four, and exhale to the count of four – one... two... three... four. Repeat this pattern for about ten breath cycles. Journal how you felt during and after.

When someone is brand new to meditation, at first things can seem overwhelming. This is because meditation techniques are on the rise and there are so many different ways to calm the mind. Focusing on your breath with exercise #6 really is the easiest way to shift your body and mind towards developing your meditative muscles. I recommend my clients do this exercise, if not daily, at least three times a week. It is also recommended that one set a timer. Begin with three minutes a day for a week, then five minutes a day for a week, adding time to each week and knowing that you are training your body and mind.

Meditation has been found to be useful for anxiety, depression, physical pain, stress, insomnia and many many other dis-eases within the body and mind. Meditation doesn't have to be lighting candles in a chakra aligned color schemed room filled with smoking incense. The breathing technique in exercise #6 can be done anywhere, anytime. When I worked law enforcement, there were many times, due to the demands of my job as officer, that I would need to sit in my patrol truck and move into this breath work. Peace of mind comes when inducing a peaceful body state or state of mindfulness.

By definition, this "mindfulness" that many have begun to seek in these chaotic times means "the quality or state of being consciously aware of something; a mental state achieved by focusing one's awareness on the present moment, while calmly acknowledging and accepting one's feelings, thoughts, and body sensations." In my workings as day to day full-time High Priestess, my mantra has become "living consciously" in all facets. This is mindfulness. The ability to stay present and not let one's focus drift too far into the planning of their future that they become overwhelmed or stressed about how they are going to accomplish that when, in actuality, it hasn't even happened yet.

Daily meditation helps us to calm the waves of our mind and emotions, helping us to focus more on the here and now rather than the 'what ifs'. When you look at animals they do not seem to be carrying a heavy load of burdens or worrying about the future. They are very good at being in the present moment. Yes ,our domestic pets do show worry, stress and upheaval but this seems to stem from the lack of proper care they are receiving by those who chose to care and provide for their needs. As humans we tend to not care and provide for our own needs, which is depleting and counterproductive to shifting our lives into a more balanced state of awareness.

There really is no right or wrong way to meditate, as long as you are entering a state of calm. As adults our brains are going, going, going all the time. We oftentimes think too much or over-think a situation so much that we create a negative situation. Taking time each day to calm the mind is a good way of gaining focus, direction and releasing negative thought patterns from not just your mental state but also your physical.

Use music to help you relax during meditation. While most find music to be comforting, it is not necessary to have the typical spa, Zen type music playing during meditation. Some prefer absolute stillness or white noise in the background. The key is to take time, if not daily then three days a week to work on developing your meditation practice. So, mix it up a bit when it comes to music styles, find what is right to you. Once you find a style or playlist that you like, use that one for a few weeks. You will find that by doing this you are training your mind and body to relax, simply by turning on your selected music. What is vital is that you make your meditation practice yours and yours alone. After all, you are an individual and there may be things that you find relaxing that others do not.

By disconnecting from the need to have only one way of doing things, or a *right or a wrong*, you open yourself up to discover who you are and what you need, how you physically and emotionally respond to your unique meditation practice. There are some who can meditate for hours, that may not be conducive to your lifestyle. Remember to not compare with others and their practice but honor the individual and authentic needs we all have.

MEDITATION EXERCISE #7

Sit in a comfortable position. Close your eyes and go back to your breath of inhaling to the count of four and exhaling to the count of four. This time, on your inhale, consciously focus on what you are breathing in; will it be calm, peace, love, healing, happiness? On your exhale consciously focus on what you are breathing out; will it be stress, fear, negative thoughts, insecurities, sorrow? Focus on just one for each inhale and exhale and, either out loud or within, state on your inhale "I breathe in _____" and on your exhale "I breathe out _____."

Clearing the mind and creating a state of calm with breath work is just the beginning. Now like the lemon exercise, we need to add messages, visualizations and prompts to help activate our subconscious to birth a more advanced tangible experience. It's time to create an intention to add to the meditation practice. For this book, the intentions in each chapter will be to activate connection with different animals and deities that have been known to mirror the particular animal's attributes. These activated connections in a meditative state will create a profound mental, emotional and physical experience as you step into the art of shapeshifting through visualization and meditation.

Guided meditation is different to self meditation as you are reliant on your meditative experience being led by someone else. Exercise #6 and #7 help you the reader to establish a baseline for your meditations. In the upcoming chapters, you may find it helpful to have someone else read the meditations to you out loud.

The guided meditations in this book consist of our baseline breath work followed by visual prompts, descriptions and messages. Just like the lemon exercise, where you focused on your breath and then mentally visualized the kitchen and experience was felt within and out. Some people are very visual and a guided meditation may be *seen* as if you were watching a movie on a screen, while others may be more auditory and may *hear* the prompts and messages but not see them vividly. Others are more kinesthetic and may *feel* what is being described in the meditation but never see it. All are good! Again, there is no right or wrong. For some, meditation may be completely new and others may be well seasoned. Just like with shapeshifting, some may be more advanced and to others this may be a completely new technique. The key really is just to embrace the possibilities.

The following exercise will help you create a safe space, an anchor or meditative space that you can go to every time you practice. This space will be where your conscious mind rests while you journey deeper into your subconscious.

MEDITATION EXERCISE #8

Sitting or lying in a comfortable position, allow your eyes to gently close and bring your focus and awareness to your breath. Breathing in 2...3...4...and exhaling out 2...3...4... (repeat several times). Allow your physical body to release all tension as you move into a more relaxed mental and physical state.

Here in this state of relaxation you are free to journey deeper into your mind. Picture yourself in a favorite place in Nature. This may be a place that you visit often, a place where you feel safe and secure. See and feel your surroundings. Connect with your surroundings. How does the ground beneath you feel? How does the air around you feel? On your next inhale, can you smell your surroundings? How do you feel being here? Allow yourself a few minutes here of connection with this space.

(Pause)

In the upcoming chapters, you can combine this exercise with the breath work of exercises #6 and #7 to amplify your meditation exercise and make the most of each guided session.

CHAPTER FIVE

MOVEMENT AND MIRROR WORK

Another activation tool for embracing shapeshifting is through movement. Each insect and animal moves their body in their own unique way. What if you gave yourself permission to mimic their movement? Would that help you connect deeper with the particular insect or animal you are embracing? Why wouldn't it? If we can tap into our childlike imagination, the possibilities are really endless. For this book we will be using yoga poses or asanas to move into a mirroring image of the particular animal or insect being discussed in each chapter.

Why is yoga such a powerful tool when activating totemism? If the definition of totemism is the ancient belief and practice of calling upon the mystical connection and relationship humans share with animals and plant life, then it only makes sense that yoga would help move this mystical relationship through the body. What better way to embody the essence of cobra than by moving your body into the cobra asana (pose). Let's face it, working with an actual live cobra seems like a very risky and unsensible way of connecting. Also one can only watch so many youtube videos and documentaries; which, although helpful, defeats the purpose of reconnecting one's self with the power of Nature.

While there is no solidified proof of the reason why the ancient yogi's named their poses after animals, it seems logical to assume that the ancient ones learned much from observing the world around them, which would include not just plant life but animals. When watching animals in their natural habitat, they encounter plenty of opportunities to fall prey or step into predator. Which, comparatively to humans, these fight or flight responses that are just a part of the animals day to day life create quite the detrimental emotional and physical dis-ease in our human lives. My guess is the ancient "people" observed that these animals were able to remain aligned and survive despite these circumstances.

As humans we have become a species weighted down by stresses, anxiety, discord, chaos and emotional highs and lows. Oftentimes one's ability to even get out of bed is crippling. How can we disconnect from these day to day stresses and step into a sense of enlightenment? What if we once again turned to Nature, plants and animals for guidance and an example of how to live in alignment?

In an article by Shannon Austin, she writes, "The busyness and high stress levels we place on ourselves prevent us from becoming aware of our bodies' sensations. It makes sense that the ancient yoga masters would have chosen to model their practice after the animals they observed – in the hopes of learning to balance their emotions and stress patterns. When we enter an animal-named pose, we both endure a physical exercise and experience a psychological exercise of embodying the symbolism of that particular animal."

This kind of consideration both physically and mentally creates a shift towards enlightenment and awareness of how we hold emotions in our body and how we can effectively move them through our own body. The next time you do a yoga pose named after an animal, consider why that particular animal moves that way.

For the purpose of this book, I have included step by step instructions to move into a yoga asana (pose) to embody the particular animal being discussed. The yoga poses are an effective way to move into the animal and connect with its individual essence. I recommend taking the yoga poses one step further and embodying them into the rituals included in each chapter as an additional way of blending physically with the individual animal in a ritual setting.

Think of what a mirror does; it reflects back to you what is looking into the mirror. Mirror work involves seeing yourself, your whole self, and learning to love that whole self. Mirror work with animals, insects or deities is seeing the attributes of those animals, insects or deities reflected back to you.

With animal totem work, the animal that comes through is not you and you are not that animal, the animal that comes through a meditation is your mirror, your reflection and reminder that you share characteristics with this particular animal. For example, for years I worked with owls. When I would look at an owl, I visualized owl as my mirror. A mirror that was showing me to activate my awareness and sight and to seek wisdom. I wasn't seeing an actual owl in the mirror as my reflection. The same goes for when I began my journey into embracing the Celtic goddess The Morrigan. When I looked into my mirror and called upon her as a guide, she did not appear to me as my reflection, rather I saw myself as having much more strength and conviction.

Louise L. Hay, who is known for developing mirror work as a method states, "Mirror work reflects back to you the feelings you have about yourself. It makes you immediately aware of where you are resisting and where you are open and flowing. Mirror work clearly shows you what thoughts you will need to change if you want to have a joyous, fulfilling life." With mirror work comes shadow work or predator work. The ability to see your WHOLE self. All of you. The good and the bad. The negative thought patterns that have physically shifted the way you perceive and see yourself. When looking at yourself in the mirror, you can't really hide from your reflection. After all, you chose to look at it. Mirror work can expose our fears AND insecurities and can bring us face to face with our inner child and our inner prey/predator. The key is perception.

How you perceive yourself is of vital importance. No matter what or how others perceive you, they only see what you allow them to see. At the end of the day, you look at yourself in the mirror. Most people who step into the "self love" movement embrace mirror work with the help of affirmations. "I am" statements designed to counteract the negative self talk that tends to fill our minds as we gaze at our reflection in the mirror. I have used affirmations for years and find them to be very helpful. With the theme of this book being anchored into animism, through shapeshifting one simply changes their affirmations. For example, a typical affirmation would be "I am strong". With changing our dialogue and applying animal terms we shift into a more instinctual and primal reflection, "I am strong like an ox."

In this practice we are calling upon insects or animals as our mirrors and asking them to reflect back to us what we already possess, we just may not have been seeing it within us. Another example is of shifting to animism through the words we speak. For example, when I was working with wolf as my primary mirror, teacher, mentor and guide, I would refer to my home as my den, my family as my pack.

Movement is a very powerful tool when combined with mirror work. Physically shifting the body can mentally shift the mind into an enhanced way of experiencing things. This practice combined with affirmations and how we talk will create an awakening of shifting perspectives and a gaining empathy of for those we call upon as our mirrors, whether they be insects, animals or deities. Along with empathy comes balance. The basic understanding and accountability of seeing and owning ones' self as whole is life changing. Whole unto one's self! One wouldn't look at a bear and judge it for being overweight or its hair too bushy. Yet we do this to each other all time in the human world. My goal with writing this book is to help create a movement and a shift back to our primal, instinctual and animal way of living, where we stop with creating boxes of expectations for others mammals like ourselves to fit into, in order for us to have empathy and kindness towards them. What if we allowed each other to have our own unique flare and be our own individual? Would society shift? What if we saw each other as animals? Would that change how we interact, how we approach, how we love?

CHAPTER SIX

ACTIVATION THROUGH RITUAL AND SPELL WORK

The dictionary tells us that "a ritual is a sequence of activities involving gestures, words, actions or objects, performed in a sequestered place and according to set sequence. Rituals may be prescribed by the traditions of a community, including a religious community."

There are many different formats for doing a ritual, many different religious organizations that have their own set of guidelines and ways of performing rituals for a many different reasons. For example, rituals are done to celebrate, commemorate and bring about change; such as childbirth, marriages, birthdays, rites of passage from one age archetype to the next (maiden-mother or knight-king), healing, blessing, feasting, fasting and so on. You can pretty much name something and create a ritual or ceremony around it.

For the purpose of this book, the rituals described in each chapter are ways of creating a tangible, physical representation of the work you are doing with the particular animal/insect and/or deity associated with it. While a ritual is not a requirement, the act of taking time to set intention, going through the process of learning about a particular insect/animal or deity is in actuality a ritual itself.

In this the book, the rituals are a way of "putting it all together" and taking what you have gained from working with a particular insect/animal or deity and honoring that connection with a ceremony.

It is also important to know that, for some, the connection through shape-shifting can be a very spiritual experience but each individual will have their own unique experience, so comparing to others is pointless and a waste of time. Instead we format and craft our own days, our own experiences and so in the following chapters there will be basic guidelines on how to prepare an altar and different ways of creating a space to do your shapeshifting in a ritual setting.

As a priestess, I love creating rituals. The entire process of gathering supplies, brewing incense and creating a physical place away from my normal day to day surroundings and then taking the time to move through that space in an intuitive way is very fulfilling to me. For me, the prepping is the main ritual and everything that follows is the icing on the cake. For this book I will break down my format for ritual, emphasizing that this is my technique and format that I have found to be useful for beginners.

Then I will offer you different ritual techniques to add to your already existing practice, if you have one.

ALTAR FOCAL POINT

Create a physical tangible space to do your ritual or shapeshifting ceremony. Or in other words, an altar. Simply put, an altar is a focal point and container for magical energies. An altar is a physical reminder of your intent, a power spot and a symbolic manifestation of your innermost self. Within the chapters of this book, an altar, if you choose to create one, is done so as an act of devotion. Humans are natural altar builders. So, chances are that you already have a couple of altars in your home. For example, maybe a book shelf or dresser top that has some of your prized possessions or objects you would describe as sacred, arranged in a particular way that has meaning to you. If you are a practicing Wiccan devoted to a specific tradition, you may already have an altar set up in a particular way according to your tradition. Keep in mind that you do NOT need to be Wiccan to shapeshift. You do not need to be a member or participant in any organized religious structure to do shapeshifting, you just need to have an open heart and open mind. There is no right or wrong way to create a physical space for shapeshifting. All you really need is a quiet room or outdoor setting where you will be uninterrupted and free from distractions. An altar is simply a physical reminder or focal point of which animal/insect or deity you are going to be working with. Oftentimes a small table works nicely. I have a wooden grocery crate that I flip over and place items on top if I am working outdoors, it has become my 'on the go' altar kit as I can place all my tools and supplies inside for easy transport. But again, an altar is not necessary, it is just nice to acknowledge in the physical world the connection and journey you are embarking upon in the mental, emotional and spiritual world.

BLESSING ONE'S SPACE

If you feel the need to move through and desire to embrace a ritual or ceremony as part of your shapeshifting, creating an energetic space free from negative energy is a good step. While most are familiar with white sage and smudging, there are numerous other ways of creating a barrier between the mundane and sacred. Smudging with sacred smoke created from burning medicinal or sacred plants is an aspect of many cultures and religions the world over. In North America it is a practice common to the indigenous peoples."

As a practicing witch for twenty-six years, I have used white sage for many years and found it to be very effective. However, as an herbalist I much prefer to use herbs that I myself have grown, dried and brewed together to create loose incense. When I first began the path of the Craft, I used simply incense as I was a teenager at the time and didn't want my parents who were Mormon to be too freaked out as white sage has a rather pungent odor. The key again is to make your experience your own always! So use whatever you desire but please do your research first as this will only empower you in creating your own authentic experience. There are many different things you can do to create sacred smoke. Once you have obtained your tool for blessing with smoke, you simply move the smoke around in a circle making sure to focus on your intention being to create sacred space. If you have set up an altar, use the smoke to smudge and clear your altar and objects upon it as well. While you are smudging in this manner you are clearing your auric field and smudging yourself.

CREATING A CIRCLE

Typically, I will begin to bless and prepare my space for ceremony by walking around it in a circle about three times. This is usually done while I am smudging the space. The altar can be placed and crafted in the center of your circle space. Why a circle? The circle is a universal symbol of containment, creating a barrier from the mundane world and the world we are creating within. There are numerous ways of creating, casting or calling in a circle for protection and to physically represent a space to do one's magic, spell, ritual or ceremony. I have been working with wolf energy for the past decade and through my observation of wolves and domesticated dogs I have found that, before they settle in to rest during the day or sleep at night, they will physically move around in a circle. We had a bloodhound named "Duchess" who had her own bed time ritual that consisted of three circles before laying down and going to sleep. Through my shapeshifting work with wolf I found that if I mirrored this walking around in a circle, sometimes on all fours, I was able to physically create a barrier and area of containment to do my ceremonies. Formulate what works and feels best for you on a physical, mental and spiritual level.

For many Wiccans devoted to a particular path or tradition there will be a different way of creating this circle or space of containment. Some practitioners call upon their ancestors, or the Watchtowers think of the movie "The Craft" and the circle they cast on the beach, for example. Some focus on the directions and begin in the east and some begin in the north. Again how you cast your circle, walk your circle or create your space is completely up to you as this is your experience and creating a circle is by no means required but the art of casting a circle can amplify your ceremony and/or ritual if you choose to embrace the ritual portion of each chapter.

WHAT IS A SPELL?

When most people hear the word spell, they immediately think back to the television series "Charmed" and picture the three sisters gathered at a podium in the attic with a large spell book sitting upon it, listing off ingredients and charms to speak to activate their magic into reality, while some think of a spell as being no different than a prayer. The dictionary defines spells as "spoken words or form of words believed to have magic power, a state of enchantment or a strong compelling influence or attraction."

For the sake of this book, a spell is simply focused intention using tangible tools and/or ingredients to bring about this focused intention into the physical world or current reality. For example, when you get to chapter seventeen and learn about cobra medicine. there is a spell included to help you call upon the protective attributes of cobra in crafting a witch's bottle.

It is important to remember that you do not need to be a witch, Wiccan or religious to gather ingredients and formulate a protective charm for your house. One just needs to believe that they possess the power to do so, and everyone has the power to protect themselves and their homes.

When I was a baby witch, casting a spell was explained to me in about the same way one explains baking a cake. Say you want to cast a spell into the Universe to attract more money; there are literally hundreds of different ingredients you can gather to add to the mix of brewing up this spell. Anything from colored candles, gemstones, coin to deities, herbs and more. The list can go on and on. The intention, however, is yours, it's personal! So, you will end up gathering items that speak to you and mean something to you. Then you will combine those ingredients and give your intention to the Universe whether in a ritual setting, cast circle or sitting at your kitchen table.

Spell work can be quite simple and it can be quite complex. But diving into spell work is not the focus of this book. So just know that in Chapter Seventeen there will be an opportunity for you to cast a spell if you have not. And if you are seasoned then hopefully it will be a spell that you enjoy.

INVOKING A DEITY

Once your space for ritual or ceremonial work is cleansed and blessed within the safety of circle containment you are ready to activate connection. For the rituals in this book, you will be able to call upon both an animal/insect and a deity. Each is chosen because of their shared attributes and each chapter the animal/insect and deity discussed mirror each other.

Have you ever wondered why the ancient ones viewed animals as holy, divine, sentient beings and then combined these qualities with gods and goddesses? For years in my solitary practice of the craft of living my life as a witch I have observed how animals and the ancients' gods are almost interchangeable. My journey into the Craft began with less structure and more Nature. Working with gods and goddesses was not something that I considered in my first decade of learning and embracing witchcraft. I began with herbalism, midwifery and healing. My early teachings happened at local veterinarian offices and observing animals giving birth. So, I understand if there is hesitation with working with the Gods from ancient pantheons.

Within in this book we will not be approaching the gods of ancient myths and legends from a viewpoint of worship. Rather we will be looking at particular gods who, in the ancient myths and legends, were seen or described as particular animals. Then we will compare, through the technique of observation, how the two share similar characteristics.

In the ritual working, you will be given invocations or prayer, chants and a calling to create the action of invoking something or someone. The invocations can be viewed as incantations, if you prefer that word.

The basic being to call upon an outside source, whether it be the essence or attributes of an animal or an ancient god, not to do the work or devotion for you, but to be your mirror. We often become confused when working with the gods from history and think that by praying, doing ritual or invoking them, we are leaning on them to do the work for us. In actuality we are simply allowing ourselves to see that we possess within us the same characteristics but sometimes we forget and need to take a long hard look in the mirror. Ritual work is oftentimes designed to be an activation.

In this book, for example, we will be calling upon wolf energy and using the Nordic goddess Skadi as "she who mirrors" the strength of a wolf. But you the practitioner will always have the choice to take bits and pieces of the brief ritual included and formulate your own ritual if you so choose.

CONNECTION THROUGH MEDITATION

With the deity and/or animal/insect invoked and welcomed into your ritual or ceremonial space, you will be given a meditation or connection activation. Being able to sit in a sacred, dedicated circle of containment, the energy vibrates with your intention and the meditations included are designed to amplify and allow you to feel the essence and vibrate the energy of the deity and/or animal/insect you are calling upon as mirror.

While first hand I know it can be difficult to enter a calm, mental and relaxed state when reading a meditation, you always have the option of having someone join you and you both take turns guiding the other through the meditation. When I read a book that has many guided meditations, I will quite often read them out loud and record them so that I can replay them.

Everyone absorbs guided meditations differently, and that is the point. We are all uniquely authentic and should be embracing that shared aspect. Whatever you need to do to make the most of your shapeshifting connection through the rituals provided will only allow you to deepen your practice and expand your progression as you shapeshifting.

LIVING CONSCIOUSLY

Part of embracing a more animistic approach to life, one's solitary practice and life perspective, is to become more aware. Nature offers us lessons, insight and guidance every day. Most of the time we are too preoccupied with distractions to see. Animism is knowing that ALL things in Nature possess their own essence, energy and soul. If we look to all animals and insects for example as teachers with a lesson to show us or new perspective, our relationship with the animal and insect changes drastically. We become more conscious of how interconnected we are despite our different species.

Nature is the ultimate Healer and the insects and animals are our greatest mirror and teachers. When out on a walk, if you stumble across a lizard, what can you learn from this encounter? Nature is always giving us opportunities to expand and grow with her. Sometimes we just need to slow down enough to absorb what she is showing us.

"Animists see the world as full of persons, both human and other-than-human, and prioritize living in conscious and respectful ways with others. These others include: animals, plants, mountains, metals, fire, bodies of water, spirits of wind and weather, deities, ancestors, star people, nature spirits, and many others. When we view animals, plants, and others as extended family, we are morally compelled to relate with them as such." – Daniel Foor Ph.D

A good way to begin to shift one's perspective is to start seeing the current relationship you have with the natural world. How do you relate to plants, animals, the Cosmos?

PUTTING IT ALL TOGETHER – HOW TO MAKE THE MOST OF THIS BOOK

Let me reiterate that I am not an expert but a constant student of life. The techniques, meditations and rituals included here are ones that I have developed and found to be helpful as I myself first began to explore shapeshifting and then later went on to teach individual clients and offer group classes.

Shapeshifting is an experience and not a religious practice. However, it has been viewed as such for decades. My motivating factor for writing this book and offering these techniques, meditations and ritual experiences is to help individuals shift back into a more animistic way of living.

Our world is in a state of chaos and division. The animals are and always have been our greatest teachers. So whether you relate more to the ancient gods and their myths and legends or the animal's attributes and examples, we can through shapeshifting combine both and once again turn to Nature as being the one thing that, as a society, unites us and we all desperately need.

Animism to me is the reminder that all things, ALL THINGS, vibrate with their own energy, essence and that all things, from the tiniest pebble, to the noxious weeds, to the smallest insect, to the largest mammal, have admirable qualities that we can honor, hold sacred and look to as DIVINE. The mindset and practice of seeing the divine in all things would make it harder for us to destroy, dispose and consume. Through embracing animism as part of our day to day lives, we can shift our mindset to a more balanced and whole way of living because we will be consciously aware of how we interact with all things. By seeing all things in Nature as alive and vibrating their own unique authenticity we begin to develop respect for all things.

By seeing through observatory eyes we begin to notice the shared similarities and the uniqueness of what we are observing. By taking time to visualize ourselves as being one with what we are observing we develop empathy. Then when we activate through movement, mirror work and meditation we begin to relate, see and feel how interconnected we really are.

The only thing that truly separates us from the plants, animals and insects is our inability to take time to connect. We create barriers of division. Some we were taught as children. For example, how many of you were taught to be afraid of spiders? How many of you were told the story of "Grandmother Spider"? Some barriers we have developed over time through embracing ego mentality and patriarchal mindsets, but all of these can shift as we are constantly shifting. The only thing ever constant is change. We can change the way we view the plants, insects, animals and the world. We can share this change in mindset and perspective and hopefully allow the future generation to be able to see just how much we can learn from the plants, insects, animals and all of Nature. For we are not separate from Nature we are very much a part of Nature. We are mammals and need to remember that our furry, four legged brothers and sisters are here to teach us, guide us and be our greatest mirrors.

This book is a guide, written to inspire and help you the reader to format your own perspectives, techniques and abilities to learn from the masters who have been on this planet much longer than we have. These master teachers, our insect and animals kin, have so much to offer us if we will only unplug and take the time to get to know them.

Donald L. Hicks says, "Those who teach the most about humanity aren't always human."

Celtic Animals
as Gods

CHAPTER SEVEN

RAVEN

INSIGHT AND NEW PERSPECTIVE

The ancient Celts were believed to be animists. They believed that many spirits; divine, sentient beings, inhabited the world around them. From rocks and plants, to elements and animals, they honored all the forces of Nature and saw that everything inhabited its own essence and energy.

They were known for their observation of animals as omens, messengers, teachers and guides. Particular animals were revered for their physical, mental and behavioral qualities. For the purposes of part two of this book, four animals well known throughout history for being linked to the early Celtic clans will each have one chapter dedicated to them, along with a brief glimpse into a Celtic god or goddess who has similar attributes to the animal, or through myth and legend has been identified and honored as *being* that animal, OR that animal *being* that particular deity.

> *"On the road to wisdom, behave like a raven*
> *and observe everything carefully!"*

MEHMET MURAT HDAN

One of several larger-bodied species of genus *corvus*. For this book we will focus on the common raven *corvus corax*, also known as the northern raven. To some, the raven is a nuisance, linked in annoyance with that of rats and mice. It is not uncommon in my desert of Southern Utah to see trash bags ripped open and trash scattered from the ravens doing what ravens do, and that is scavenge.

In Scandinavia, ancient Ireland, Wales, Northwest Coast of North America, Siberia and Northeast Asia the common raven has been, and still is, revered as a spiritual figure or godlike creature. If one was to google "shapeshifting gods" the top deity to appear would be the Celtic goddess The Morrigan, whom we will discuss in depth a bit later.

Ravens are quite large in size, unlike their cousin the crow, which are much smaller. Ravens also communicate differently than crows. For example, crows make a "ka ka" sound, while ravens have a deep croak. Ravens are much larger in stature, wing span and their feathers and beak are very different from that of crows. For this book, we will be working with raven and saving crow for another volume.

Ravens are incredibly smart, having one of the largest brains of any bird species, particularly the part of the brain called the hyperpallium which is linked to vision.

On a metaphysical level, ravens like most birds are symbolic of taking flight, or seeing what has "flown" into your life. In healing sessions, when a bird comes through, I utilize that energy to rise above and begin to see things with a new perspective. Ravens see into the secrets of one's soul which is why they are linked to magic and the occult. Their eyes much like equines are mirrors. Raven energy can be intense, with a hint of mystery.

MEDITATION EXERCISE #9

Close your eyes and bring your awareness to your breath. Allow your physical body to relax, all the way from your forehead to your toes. Give yourself permission to move down through your body and release any tension you may have on your exhales. With your eyes gently closed, free your mind of wandering thoughts and tap into your imagination.

Take your time and slowly think of ravens. You may see ravens flying around you, perched beside you or you may even be shifting into raven. Whatever your subconscious decides to do is right. See raven, the shimmering almost metallic shine of dark black feathers with hints of blues and greens. Focus in on one particular raven and really see how it begins to observe its surroundings. Watch as it cocks its head almost mechanically in a tick tick tick motion. This raven slowly and meticulously looks directly at you. It's eyes dark brown. Gazing at you, your eyes lock and you see your reflection mirrored back. Raven is studying you. Seeing into the very depths of your soul which you try so painstakingly to hide. Raven sees what's underneath. It is natural when your darkest depths are exposed to look away, which you do. Raven simply cocks its head, kicks up with its talons and rises up. Its wings spanning wide; it slowly circles, this time watching you from above. It circles once, then twice and then flies away. Bring your awareness back to your breath and back to the present, the here and now.

Journal prompts – take time to journal about your experience with raven. Did you see a raven? Did the raven see you? How deeply did it see?

Ravens, like all animals, are messengers. Animals in general are instinctual which, as mammals, humans should be too. But we have learned to second guess ourselves, to talk ourselves out of something and to doubt, resist and argue with our guttural instincts. What if we were to rise above the need to rationalize and compromise ourselves and soar into activating change in our lives by trusting our first gut reaction? Ravens and birds show us just how to fly up above our worries, doubts and insecurities and either swoop in and take charge or simply soar for a bit until the time is right.

Ravens are also scavengers. When a raven shows up in your life, or when you are ready to call upon and shift into raven energy, you may have to dig down through the layers you used as protection and be exposed, oftentimes in an uncomfortable way. The act of allowing parts of you to surface through turmoil can be referred to as a 'rebirthing'. Maybe raven energy is just what you need. This scavenger ability to feed on the dead and find sustenance could also be a mirror to you that it's time to adjust your perspective.

Feeding on the dead is a statement that, if given time to digest and look at with new eyes, can open up many new doors. After all, it's our view of things that really determines how we will act or react. So, if you are ready to dive into raven magic and embrace the essence of ravens, please do so with *open eyes and keen insight.*

As creatures that feast on the dead, ravens in myths, legends and lore have been linked with the otherworld, underworld and the beyond. They are seen as omens of illness, death, bad luck and gateway keepers between the living and the dead.

In Swedish folklore they are the ghosts of murdered people who did not have a Christian burial. In some stories from Germany they were souls that had been damned. In Greek mythology ravens are said to be bad luck.

According to the mythological narration, Apollo sent a white raven, or crow in some versions, to spy on his lover, Coronis. When the raven brought back the news that Coronis had been unfaithful to him, Apollo scorched the raven in his fury, turning the animal's feathers black. That's why all ravens are black today.

In the Welsh Mabinogian the raven is the harbinger of death. One could ask if the death so feared is literal or metaphorical. Or could it just be that raven is croaking at you to look at this "death" with a new perspective as well?

In the wild ravens are messengers to others animals as well. Ravens often will lead wolves to carcasses as well as other predators looking for a meal.

This idea of seeing something dark and ominous with new eyes leads me to the great Celtic Queen The Morrigan who is often times depicted as a raven. She too is seen as dark and ominous. In fact, years ago, when I first embraced The Morrigan, I felt it was a good idea for my Coven to dedicate to her as a whole for the next year. It was rather annoying all the "warnings" that appeared in my research. Pretty much most of what I read was "do not work with the Morrigan, she will conquer and destroy your life."

The Morrigan has many names and titles. I could devote an entire book to any deity really that I have personally worked with, but that is not the intent with this book. Plus there are amazing books dedicated to The Morrigan my most recent favorite being "The Morrigan: Celtic Goddess of Magick and Might by Courtney Weber." Another favorite being "Feast of The Morrighan by Christopher Penczak." My intention with this book is to help each reader see the connection between Divine beings such as the Morrigan and divine creatures such as ravens.

One such title of The Morrigan's that has always stood out to me is "Lady of Ravens." She being the top most common result upon researching shapeshifting deities. The Morrigan is also known as Goddess of War, Fate and Death. She is the Great Queen. The Celts believed that, as they engaged in warfare, The Morrigan flew shrieking overhead in the form of a raven or carrion crow, summoning a host of slain soldiers to a macabre spectral bane. When the battle had ended, the warriors would leave the field until dawn in order that The Morrigan could claim the trophies of heads, euphemistically known as "The Morrigan's acorn crop." Is the Morrigan one who truly shapeshifts her physical form into that of a raven. Or did the ancient Celts have a deeper respect for Nature and animals? Did they honor this sacred bird as Divine? Were all animals "godlike?"

The Morrigan is one who foretells doom, death, victory or upcoming battle. I think of her as a messenger, much like ravens. What is she conveying or asking me to see with a new perspective and keener eyesight?

When I hear her referred to as the "Battle Queen", I internalize that and look at her as a mirror of what am I battling or in need of fighting and ultimately conquering or do I need to lay down my sword and submit?

Raven energy is much the same. Ravens are unpredictable; they are like all wild animals. They trust their instincts. I have observed my little raven family challenge other birds in our yard. One of the larger 'teenage' ravens decided it would go after one of the songbirds' nests that were in our tree we fondly call "Sarah". The song bird was not going to tolerate that and, together with about three other songbirds, began to frantically dart at and peck the much larger raven. I believe this raven could have easily taken on the smaller birds but it picked its battle and after much persistence from the songbirds the raven retreated.

Life itself is one big mirror. I feel it just depends on who is reflecting back to us what we need to see or usually will resist seeing?
I know animal medicine to be an effective and much needed tool. My goal is to help people see that the only disconnect we have with animals is our belief that humans are superior and that they have dominion over the

animals. In essence, animals are the greatest teachers, messengers and mirrors.

The ancient people knew this, saw this and had a much deeper more meaningful relationship with animals than most do today. I truly believe this practice of respect and adoration is what linked animals with "godlike" attributes and the animals in turn became reflections of the gods.

As one of Scottish, Irish and English bloodlines, I have always felt at home with the Celtic deities and Celtic magick traditions, but The Morrigan had a fearful reputation. One that I honestly wanted to approach with caution. When the ravens began to visit my property I could have ignored them, but as a priestess of this goddess, I looked at this opportunity as a gift and sacred responsibility from the Raven Queen herself to learn to honor, care for and respect with gratitude *"her"* birds. *Her* other form. This is not a responsibility that I take lightly.

Ravens being highly intelligent birds not only remember faces of those who feed them, but they remember faces of those who have wronged them. In fact, studies have shown that Ravens and Crows can and will react to human faces linked to both stressful and positive situations for up to five years.

Most people have read the story of the little girl who was given presents, shiny objects by crows. This is a little girl who leaves food out for the crows in her garden and in return they bring her gifts.

"The Girl Who Gets Gifts from Birds" by Katy Sewall

https://www.bbc.com/news/magazine-31604026

MEDITATION EXERCISE #10 – TO CONNECT WITH THE MORRIGAN

To begin with please close your eyes and focus on your breath. Take a nice deep inhale and exhale fully. Breathe in and breathe out. Just continue this pattern, allowing each muscle and cell to relax with each exhale. Allow your mind to clear, your fears and apprehensions to be released as you exhale. Pushing out with your breath that which no longer serves you. Now breathe in 2...3...4...and out 2...3...4... (repeat three times)

In your mind's eye see yourself sitting on a grassy knoll, feel the damp, crisp cool air of the Green Island. For some of you this may feel like home, for others this may feel like foreign land, but this is a safe space, filled with ancient magic. So ancient, the dirt itself seems alive. Sitting here, absorbing the scenery, it feels as if everything around you is alive. Pulsating with its own unique energetic thread all woven together to create this earth.

Sitting here, you see down at the bottom of the hill a hooded figure, robed in black. Above a raven, large and mysterious soars. To some this may seem an odd couple, but not here in that ancient land of magick. This site is all too familiar. As the figure removes the hood of the robe you notice it is a woman, with hair the color of midnight, eyes deep and piercing. She needs no introduction for her legend precedes her. The raven swoops down and gracefully lands on her shoulder and they slowly make their way up the hill to where you are sitting. Your instinct may be to stand to show honor but something keeps you seated on the grass. Almost instantly she is sitting next to you and you are both watching her raven fly overhead.

You turn your head to look at her and find she is already staring deeply into your eyes, piercing deep into your soul. She sees past your exterior shield and is seeing the real you, the one that you keep hidden, the one that you may be afraid of, embarrassed of or even unaware of. She sees you. With eyes like a raven she sees your authentic self.

It is normal to feel uneasy or emotional when interacting with the Great Queen called The Morrigan. For her reputation is one meant to frighten and intimidate. Take a few deep breaths here and feel her energy, hear her words.

(Pause)

The Morrigan helps you to your feet and asks you to hold out your hands. She places a small sword in your right hand and places her other hand over your heart. "This sword represents strength and power to cut through the issues, doubts and fears that you have placed before you. With my other hand I bless you with self love, for all healing must start within first."

Next The Great Phantom Queen takes a knife from her belt and pierces her finger until you see a droplet of bright red blood forming. She then takes her finger and places it on your lips, you can taste the salty sweetness of her blood. "This is a reminder that you too have within you the blood of ancients, my blood, the bloodlines of the ancient ones. I have gifted you with more blood, the blood of my ancient ancestors. May it infuse you with remembrance for that which is remembered lives."

The Morrigan picks up what appears to be a robe and places it around your shoulders. She takes your hands in hers and kisses the palms of each hand. In return you do the same, kissing her palms with tears running down your face onto her skin. Right before your eyes she transforms herself into a large raven and soars away.

Take a deep breath in and really allow yourself to soak in this gift that was given by one so powerful.

(Pause)

Allow the emotions to rise, allow yourself to feel.

(Pause)

See yourself slowly walking down the grassy knoll. Down at the bottom you notice there is a small creek flowing. You place your robe and sword on the ground and lay yourself in the creek, it is surprisingly warm. Think of all the self doubts, insecurities and fears that consume you and prevent you from living the most authentic life. Feel the water carry them away.

When you are cleansed, slowly leave the creek, put back on the robe and pick up your sword, lick your lips and taste the sweet, salty blood of the Great Queen and remember you too are sovereign and must reign supreme in your own kingdom/queendom.

CREATING A RITUAL TO CONNECT WITH RAVEN AND THE MORRIGAN

Altar suggestions: cloth of red or black to be used as an altar cloth or table cloth. Items that represent the directions if you choose to do a circle casting. East-feathers, south-candles, west-bowl, chalice or cauldron, north-stones.

In the center, a picture of a raven or The Morrigan would complete the altar, along with a candle. For it will be The Morrigan that we will be calling upon to help us activate and awaken the ability to shift and shape.

Creating the container: or casting your circle to separate the mundane world and the spiritual. When I am leading public rituals, my circle casting can be quite intricate. For this solitary beginning you can simply address each direction by placing the directional objects onto the altar. Once the directions are welcomed it is time to light the raven/Morrigan candle in the center and call upon her.

INVOCATION TO THE LADY OF RAVENS, THE MORRIGAN

"We call to The Morrigan, Great Queen, Lady of Ravens, she who shifts between the worlds, the species and the beyond. We call to your sacred birds the ravens. Those who are both mysterious and intelligent. We welcome their new perspectives and insights as we begin the journey of shapeshifting, as we go into the dark of our souls, where the ability to become one with all animals sits. We call to you with humility and deep respect and vow to honor this gift and not only shift our conscious awareness but our entire life towards a knowing and practice that we are not apart from Nature that we are a part of it. That we are not separate from our animal siblings, we are one with them and honor them as our teachers, messengers and mirrors. So mote it be."

MEDIATION EXERCISE #11

Begin by taking your awareness back to your meditative breath. Close your eyes and begin to visualize. Allow your physical body to be in an upright sitting position and in your mind's eye, visualize yourself sitting outside on a warm sunny day beneath a tall tree, and slowly begin to cock your head in a slow and strategic manner. Feel as your breath exhales from your nose which begins to shift into that of a beak. Adjust to this new sensation of breathing through a beak which is long, hard and pointed. Allow yourself to cock your head downward and connect your beak with the ground, pressing your now beak into the grass. Feel as the weight of your body begins to shift and become smaller and lighter. Feeling this weight shift from your upper body down to your lower body where your legs and feet become talons with sharp piercing claws on rough scaled legs.

Feel as your upper body moves lower to the ground. Stretching your arms out to the side they begin to morph into wings, feathers of dark shiny black. Your entire body is now that of raven. Breathe that in. Breathe in the mystery and intellect of this wise bird. Feel yourself begin to move upon the ground, almost in a hopping manner you move your taloned feet. Ready to lift up you dig your talons into the grass. Holding the dirt you kick up off the ground. With your wings outstretched, you lift up, higher and higher until you are soaring. Feel as your body is weightless but supported by the air currents that allow you to glide. Gazing below at the tree that you were seated beneath, you cock your head and see things with new eyes, new perspective. This is the power of raven to rise above your turmoil and look for new direction. In this moment just glide. Soar and enjoy the connection with being one with raven.

Slowly bring yourself back down to the ground. Bring your focus back to your breath. Begin to stretch your talons until they become human feet once more and feel your legs, feet and entire body shifting back to form. Feel your entire body shaking off the raven feathers and revealing your skin beneath.

Activating your internal organs with your breath, you do the same with your face, feeling your beak become small, flesh covered, along with your lips, eyelids and cheeks. Breathing in your whole, complete and invigorated form completely back to that of human. Giving yourself pause to hold on and anchor into the new perspectives and insight that flying as raven provided, begin to wiggle your fingers and toes and, taking one last breath in, you open your eyes and are ready to begin.

You can now snuff out the candle on your center altar, offering gratitude. If you wish you can release the directions that you called in and of course journal your experience as raven.

There are many ways to activate and enhance your connection with animals. You can observe them in their natural habitat, go through a meditative experience as mentioned before or you can move your body into similar physical stances or poses of the individual animal you are working with. As a yoga instructor, I have learned that most asanas (yoga poses) mimic animals. Utilizing yoga helps in a physical meditation when calling upon the animal of your choosing.

Physically we believe that we are limited. However, if you look at the practice of yoga, almost all poses reflect that of an animal. Why? I believe it is because the ancients allowed themselves that connection with animals as students. When one begins a yoga practice, things internal as well as external begin to shift and move. One's overall health, stamina, strength and endurance are all activated in a positive way.

My journey with yoga began nineteen years ago when I was pregnant with my second child. I was planning my first home birth and wanted to be both physically and emotionally prepared, yoga seemed like the solution. Since then I have been both a student and teacher of yoga. When my second child was two, I began to teach partner yoga at a local gym and since then I have not been consistent in my yoga practice. Until December 1st of 2018, when I made a commitment to do yoga every day, every day! It is now early 2019 and I am in my second year of this commitment and I feel a change both internally and out.

When embracing raven through yoga, there is a pose called Bakasana or "crow pose." This is an intimidating arm balance with a variety of health benefits. In appearance, the body looks like a crow/raven perched and about to lift off the ground and take flight. Physically, this pose strengthens the wrist, forearms and abdomen while stretching the upper back. It improves balance and core strength. Which, speaking chakra language, one's core is the home of the solar plexus which is the seat of confidence. Crow pose is as much a mental challenge as it is a physical challenge. Your brain wants to tell you that you are going to face plant the ground. My best suggestion that I give to my students is similar to that of working with The Morrigan; you have to disconnect from your ego, that seat of doubt, fears and insecurities. You have to trust your body and let go. Reassure yourself repeatedly that you can "do this!"

Just like a baby raven has to just trust that when they kick off the branch for the first time their wings and the air current are going to lift them up, with this pose it's mental as much as physical.

EMBRACING RAVEN ENERGY THROUGH PHYSICAL MOVEMENT

Step by step instructions to move into crow/raven pose:

- Begin in a standing position, palms together.
- Inhale and reach both arms up, getting a nice stretch and coming down into a forward bend.
- From this forward bend you can bend your knees if necessary and, placing your palms flat on the ground, you then come down into a comfortable squat position.
- With knees pointed out and your hands flat in front of you about a foot from your body, you gently rest your knees onto your triceps and begin to shift your body weight forward onto your wrists and hands.
- In this position, you are almost ready to pick up your feet and hold the pose.

If you are worried about falling forward, which is a common fear, you can place a pillow on the ground in front of you, but ultimately remember you are not far off the ground. Go slow and remember to breathe.

This is a great pose to use when wanting to step into raven energy. It is excellent for building mental discipline and activating your body, mind intellect. This pose increases mental focus and calm.

When preparing for shapeshifting to that of raven, this pose will help tremendously. Create your container, cast your circle and after lighting your candle go into crow/raven pose and breathe raven energy into your body. From here you can focus on what it is you are in need of from harnessing raven energy.

For example, are you in assistance of retaining information for an upcoming exam? Are you wanting a new perspective before tackling a current situation, job or other obstacle? Or do you simply want to stimulate connection with raven and open yourself up to receive whatever message or medicine raven has to offer? Either way, by positioning your physical body into that of raven, you are one step closer to shifting the shape of things.

When you first begin to acknowledge the power of shifting energy with animals the key is to be aware. Not cautiously aware, just open to see, receive and obtain the information being given by animals.

In Ted Andrews book, "Animal Speak: The Spiritual and Magical Powers of Creatures Great and Small" he states, "Animals speak to those that listen."

CREATING A SPACE IN YOUR YARD FOR RAVENS

If you are living in an area where ravens are prominent, you can physically takessteps to invite them into your yard so that you can observe them better. Please speak to your local aviary expert or wildlife official first to make sure it is legal, as quite a few neighborhoods may not appreciate you welcoming ravens and their scavenging ways.

https://birdeden.com/how-to-attract-crows-to-your-backyard

CHAPTER EIGHT

HORSE

STRENGTH AND STAMINA

"For one to fly, one needs only to take the reins."

MELISSA JAMES

Horses are well known in myths and legends as having supernatural abilities and magical attributes. Epona is just one! Odin in Norse mythology for example rode upon an eight-legged horse Sleipnir. There are images and carvings found in stone that date back as far as the 8th century.

Horses are a symbol of freedom. When you think of a wild stallion running free with no restraints, it ignites a passion inside to be that free. It's sad to think that in order for a horse to be manageable it has to be "broken". Horses that are trained and broken to follow their leader/owner out of respect are much more enjoyable and happier than those who are made to follow out of fear. This can be mirrored in humans as well. Again, we need to re-examine the mirrors being shown to us by animals in order to shift our shaping of them.

Around 1950, equine therapy began to gain popularity. Research has shown that equine-assisted therapy is effective for PSTD, depression, anxiety, autism, dissociative disorders, ADHD and other mental health conditions.

Horses are particularly known for reducing anxiety and depression and studies have shown that animal-assisted therapy reduces cortisol, the stress hormone. In addition, spending time with animals lowers blood pressure. It also increases the release of oxytocin, a natural chemical that promotes feelings of positivity and connection.

While all animals see into your depths, there is something about a horse. They are bullshit meters. If you are scared of them they will sense that. Paulo Coelho says, "The eyes are the mirror of the soul and reflect everything that seems to be hidden; and, like a mirror, they also reflect the person looking into them." When you apply this to animal magick and shapeshifting you are calling upon the particular animal you are working with and utilizing "its" way of seeing.

Did you know that horses have some of the largest eyes of any land mammal? With moose having the largest. A horses eyes are situated on the side of their heads which gives them a wide range of vision. They can see nearly 360 degrees and have blind spots only immediately in front and immediately behind their bodies.

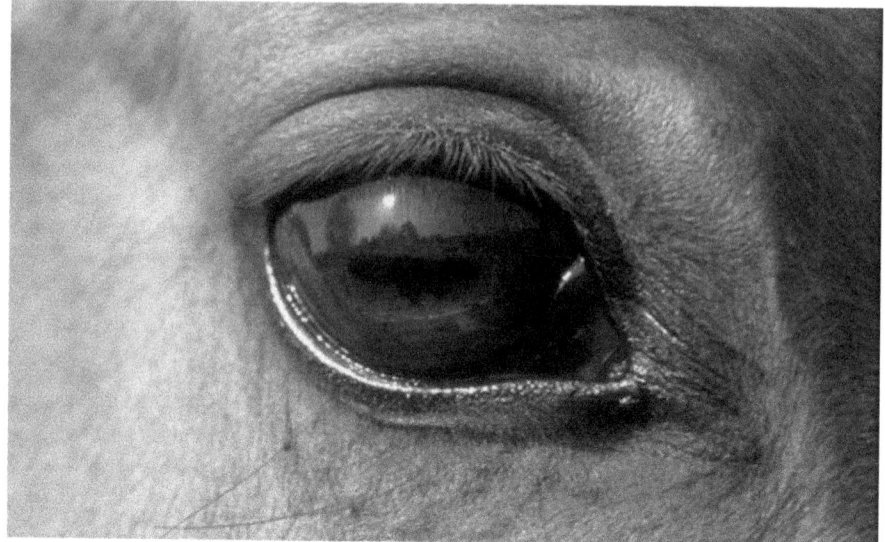

Horses use mostly monocular vision – meaning both eyes are used separately. So a horse can see and process different things happening on different side of her body. However, a horse can also use binocular vision when looking ahead.

Just like we did with the raven meditation, when it comes to calling in an animal's energy, you are simply entering ritual or meditation space. That space that lies between your ego brain and your subconscious. You give yourself permission to relax the conscious and step into the depths of your subconscious. In this state your subconscious becomes a sponge and your physical body will react to the messages given to you in the meditation.

MEDITATION EXERCISE #12 – HORSE

We always begin with our breath. Giving yourself permission to go within and relax both mentally and physically. Taking a nice deep inhale and exhaling fully. Allowing your eyelids to gently close and going back to that rhythm of breathing in to the count of four and exhaling out to the count of four. Repeat this breathing pattern seven times. Drift into a comfortable state of relaxation and just like with raven and the lemon, begin to tap into your mind's eye, your seat of imagination, and picture yourself standing in a field.

As you gaze around you at this field, you can see the wildflowers nodding in the gentle breeze, you feel the warmth of the sun on your face and you began to feel a very strong sense of calm. Standing in this field, you see that you are not alone. A majestic tan colored horse is also standing in this field.

Having been spotted by the horse, it slowly begins to walk towards you, each step precise. As it walks your way its massive head slowly nods up and down. Its mane of black moving ever so slightly with the breeze.

Your ego says to be afraid of this very large, wild horse approaching you but instead you disconnect from that old pattern of thinking and remember that you have chosen to visit this field today with the intent to connect with horse energy. So, you simply calm your breathing and allow horse to approach.

With great caution and intimidating size, the horse now stands directly in front of you. Its large nostrils flare as it breathes you in. Its eyes observe every inch of you in an almost unnerving manner. You do nothing but allow this connection. You give the horse permission to really see you, and in doing so, you look into its eyes and see yourself.

There is a stillness and immediate calm that sets in as the horse simply moves around you. It is not bothered by you and you are not bothered by it. But yet you both share this field. There is an understanding and profound respect with as horse connects with you. A sensation that you honor and agree to utilize in your day to day connections with everyone you come into contact with.

You watch as the horse slowly begins to walk away from you. Observing you one last time with a glance back, it begins to trot away. You are standing alone in the field.

Bring your awareness back to your breath. Creating that pattern once more of breathing in to four counts and out to four counts. You slowly begin to breathe back into this conscious realm with each inhale infusing your body back to the present.

Journal prompts: How can you implement the silent strength of horse into your daily life? Can you be strong within your own knowing that you do not need to project onto others but simply allow?

THE CELTIC GODDESS EPONA – PROTECTRESS OF HORSES

As with The Morrigan, there are many books and practitioners devoted to Epona. I encourage you to digest and absorb as much as information as you can on any deity that you choose to embrace. But ultimately, the connection you formulate based on your research and time spent will determine your own definition and relationship with the deity you are embracing. Take your time!

The name Epona comes from the Celtic "epos" meaning "horse" and the suffix "ona" affixed means "on". Epona is known as the Goddess of Mares (female horses) and Foals (young horses). Depictions and inscriptions of Epona have been found in North-Eastern Gaul, the Rhine region, Rome, Germany and Danubian provinces, just to name a few. These almost always feature Epona with a horse by her side, her riding on a horse or two horses on each side of her.

There are many shrines in her honor, most of which can be found in stables and temples. As Protectress of Mares and Foals, it only makes sense that the ancient peoples would call upon her and craft these shrines much like we do in our homes when working with a specific Deity or God to bless our spaces, spells and/or other needs.

If we look to the Gods and animals as teachers that mirror to us how we should live than it only makes sense that Epona is showing us how to care for, honor and respect horses.

Then you need to look at the Celts and their relationship to horses. The horse has always been highly regarded. A prized symbol of one's status, they were to be treated with great respect and honored. When the warriors would inscribe with woad dye symbols or sigils onto their horses, it was done as a way of offering protection to not only the horse but the rider.

Nature and all its "parts" has always been the closest I have felt to any Divine Being(s). From plants as allies and healing friends to animals, these have godlike attributes, but animals especially. It is my belief that the ancient people had such a respect and devotion for the Nature that they relied upon for their very survival, that the animals that assisted them, fed them and showed them how to survive, were "gods" and throughout time the legends of gods and animals became one and the same, interchangeable.

When you are seeking connection to a deity and are struggling, maybe you should consider reaching out to that deity through the animal associated with them?

RITUAL CONNECTION WITH THE
GODDESS EPONA

While structure is valued for some in their solitary practice, others have found that an intuitive flow and riding those waves of the "liminal spaces" (as Laura Tempest Zakroff describes in her book, "Weaving the Liminal") can oftentimes create more of an impact. The below is a simple guideline to help you as you journey meditatively towards a more meaningful and intent oriented connection with Epona as horse.

Altar set up: green cloth, to represent abundance and earth energy. Chalice and/or bowl, offering plate, fresh flowers, braided hair, picture or figurine of a horse or the Goddess Epona.

Blessing the space: this can be done before you even set your altar, however and whatever herbs you use to smudge with and whatever liquid you use for blessing. Our ritual took place in June so I smudged with mugwort and used moon water for the water blessing. You can also use herbal tea, which is nice.

Casting your circle: this is your ritual, so create your container to hold your magick however you wish. I have attended public and private rituals and some circle castings are very elaborate, poetic, intense, some in foreign languages, others short and sweet. Do what feels right to you always. Some begin in the north and others in the east. We are mammals and need to get back to trusting our gut responses and inclinations.

Call to the Goddess Epona: once you have called and welcomed or summoned the directions, earth below and sky above, you can call to the Goddess.

INVOCATION TO EPONA

"Divine Mare, Horse Mother, She who is the sigil of silent strength. She who brings protection, healing and prosperity to all. Great Horse. Proud to run free in your authenticity. Gazing into your mirrored eyes I see myself, hungry for the same freedom and I see reflected back only love.

No judgement, only love.

I ask for your protection great mother. I ask for healing and prosperity within. I ask for your sacred horse as mirror and teacher that I may nurture and awaken my intuition, understanding and remember that I too am a mammal, capable of trusting my instincts. So mote it be!"

MEDITATION EXERCISE #13

Here in the spaces of the in between, allow yourself to settle in. Getting into a comfortable position or horse pose (mentioned below) and, when you are ready, allowing your eyes to gently close. Bringing awareness to your breath, inhaling to the count of four and exhaling to the count of four. Repeat this breathing pattern over and over again, until you are ready to tap into your mind's eye. Disconnecting from outside thoughts that may be limiting and trusting the process, you begin to imagine that you are in the field once more. This time you are on all fours. You can feel the ground beneath your hands and knees. Even with your toes curled under, you connect with the dirt and anchor into that earth base. Breathing down into your limbs, you feel hooves beginning to replace what were your hands, legs and feet. While you still remain on all fours your limbs have lengthened into strong muscular, lean and toned legs of a horse. Your center is a mass of muscles, tight and firm. Your neck is elongated and your entire face has moved out and up, becoming horse from the ground up.

You breathe in deep, deeper than you have ever inhaled before, maybe because your nostrils can take in so much more air. You pivot your ears side to side and can hear with such intensity. Your muscles spasm with each breath as you connect with this body, the body of horse. You pick up one hoof at a time and with much vigor you increase your speed, picking up one at a time until you are trotting. Moving in a way you have never moved before, you trot around the field.

Allowing yourself time to move such a large massive body, you begin to move quicker, into a full-on gallop. You feel the mane of your hair and the whipping of your tail as you move and the air moves through each strand. This is freedom. To be one with your physical form and to celebrate the way that it moves. You have been so engrossed in galloping and playing with this new horse body that you haven't noticed the other horse in the field. A stunning white/cream colored mare begins to trot towards you. Her head is held high and there is an intimidating strength and show of pride as she moves towards you, but her gaze is soft and gentle. The Goddess Epona slows her stride and walks right next to you. Her large midsection brushing up against yours, she nudges you with a subtle yet effective bump. She moves her large head towards yours and gives you an additional nudge. She is encouraging you to play. She is reassuring you that you are safe to move forward, backwards, in circles...Whichever direction you need to go. She wants you to know that you are safe. She will protect you, though you will not need her protection. She slowly begins to move away from you and you follow. It is not long before you are both trotting, slow and precise. Moving forward in a more determined manner, you both gallop. As your gallop speed increases so does the stride of your legs and you are running. Running as fast as you can. Your hooves kicking up dirt clods as you go.

There is nothing holding you back. You are free! Wild and uninhibited. Don't give up! Don't stop! Keep running. Go where ever the wind takes you. Feel that sense of freedom! Remember you are not alone.

(Pause)

Bringing your awareness back to your breath, you begin to slow your run, taking it back to a gallop and slow trot. Slowing down but not forgetting the freedom that you just felt. The Great Mother Mare Epona nods her head in approval and you breathe back down into your limbs. Feeling them once more becoming your hands, your knees and your feet. You breathe your awareness back into your physical human form all the way from your head to your feet, taking a moment to adjust and reconnect with yourself as whole and free.

Journal your experience.

Besides meditation, shapeshifting, ritual and one-on-one connection with horse, you can move horse energy down and through your body utilizing yoga. Yes there is a horse yoga pose. This particular pose is a standing pose that strengthens the muscles in your legs and creates more flexibility in your inner thighs. Horse pose is an excellent way to build toned strong legs. Horse pose also helps with improving awareness and improving your alertness. You can hold the pose or you can bounce slowly up and down to create dynamic movement and ultimately go deeper into the stretch.

Step by step instruction for horse pose:

- Get into a standing position and step your feet out slightly wider than shoulder distance, point your toes out.
- Inhale and raise your arms up, reaching high towards the ceiling.
- Exhale and bring your hands together, lowering them over your heart. While you do this you bend your knees coming into what feels like a squat, only you do not let your knees go over your toes.
- Keep knees and feet pointed out to the side and tuck your tailbone in.
- Hold for three deep breaths.

In moments where you need a reminder of how free horse energy is, you can reconnect with your breath, hold horse pose and watch this youtube video:

https://youtu.be/5gq7no2ZQC

"In all things of nature there is something of the marvelous."

ARISTOTLE

Something shifted in our society when we became influenced or rather brainwashed with the concept of having "dominion over all the earth and over every creeping thing that creeps on the earth." Animals became our property, something to stake a claim upon. "Beasts of burden." We forgot that animals were revered, honored and worshipped as supreme beings, teachers, messengers and viewed as gods. It's time to re-shift, re-think and undo centuries of damaged thinking. Now more than ever we need to heal our relationship with the Earth because we need her! Our existence depends on her! One simple step is to heal our relationship with animals. They do not belong to us! We belong to them. If any of you own a cat, you will understand what I am saying. I always tell people who come to visit that we are all guests in my pet's home. Animals are far superior to us in so many ways. I will never forget the healing that took place that day with the horses. It was as if years of unhealthy and incorrect dogma were finally cleared from not only my psyche, but everyone who was in attendance. There is a marvelous grace in all things of nature we just have to be willing to reconnect with it.

Shapeshifting gives us the tool, it's not a new tool by any means. The ancient ones worked with animals naturally. We are in a state of consciousness where we are wanting a deeper meaning to life and we are seeking ways to call in that connection and power that the ancient ones had and, looking back through history, it seemed so effortless. Now we have to really set intentions, create time and focused energy to activate our "reconnection" with Nature. Now, more than ever, is the time to heal what was broken when we as a society embraced dominance and ownership over animals.

CHAPTER NINE

DEER

MEDICINE AND MAGICK

"INSTINCTUAL AND WISE"

"I'm always with you even if you can't see me. I'm here."

BAMBI'S MOTHER

Deer are known for being skittish but also protective. Deer medicine, messages and magick are all about focusing on and acknowledging senses. Deer have quite large ears, meaning they can hear very acutely. They also have very large watchful eyes. Deer in the forest are usually alerted of danger by birds, and then they go on to alert.

Typically we tend to rationalize and justify the actions that we take. Very rarely do we tap into our gut instincts and act accordingly. Deer are very sensitive and graceful. Author Elena Harris says, "By affinity with this animal, you have the power to deal with challenges with grace. You master the art of being both determined and gentle in your approach. The deer totem wisdom imparts those with a special connection with this animal with the ability to be vigilant, move quickly, and trust their instincts to get out of the trickiest situations."

You are more likely to be killed by a deer than you are a bear, shark or even a dog. Statistics show that around 120 people a year are killed in deer-related incidents. So it goes to say that when honoring or working with deer, there is a heightened level of respect.

When looking at deer as mirror or messenger, along with the reminder that you are actually more in tune than you want to believe; you are also a force and capable of tackling any task that you may be facing.

Deer have a wide field of vision. This is because of the placement of their eyes. They can see to the side of them, whereas we humans have to turn our head. A deer's sense of smell is 10,000 times better than the average human. Making their sense of smell their most heightened sense. A deer can smell a human a half mile away. This is why, to me, seeing this herd of deer so close and they did not fear me was a gift! Deer can also process up to six different smells at one time. You would think that, because of their large ears, deer actually hear the same that we do. They can however pick up on foreign sounds that do not belong in their area, which alerts them to danger. In one way they can hear what we don't. Their ears pick up on high frequency sounds again alerting them to possible danger. While their hearing might not be "better" than a human their range of hearing is greatly improved due to the mobility of their ears. When applying this as a mirror one could easily ask "what if I tapped into really listening? Or what if I focused on sniffing through the bullshit and seeing what is coming at me from either side?" We can tap into animals' essence by simply applying their attributes the best we can into how we go about our day to day activities. How we problem solve and even better how we react to a current situation we are facing.

Deer have always been revered as calm and serene. We have quite a few deer herds where we live and for the most part they are calm. But they are like any animal and will protect and defend by force if they feel threatened. By working with animals as our mirrors, we give ourselves permission to embrace our senses and become more instinctual. From personal observations, I have seen that this instinct to flee or stay and defend is drastically declining amongst the human population. We are quick to defend online in social media forums but are we really interacting with others on a personal level? A level that allows us to feel energies and trust our guts to let us know if we should stick around or leave? Have we as humans checked out and moved away from our animal instincts? Have we forgotten that we are animals? In a world full of computers, smart phones, texting, instant messages, Facebook profiles, blocking, unfriending...And on and on.....Are we really engaging with each other enough to be able to relate and gain appreciation for or against? How can we actually tap into our senses to alert us when we are separated by a screen?

MEDITATION TO CONNECT WITH DEER

This meditation is best done outside in a quiet park, forest or yard. Please leave your electronic devices elsewhere and allow yourself time to really be out in Nature. Once outside sitting or laying in a comfortable position, close your eyes and focus on your breath. Allow yourself to create a rhythm and flow with each inhale and exhale. Disconnect from the tendency for your mind to wander and allow yourself connection with the elements around you. With your eyes closed, move your awareness to your ears. Really allow yourself to hear all the sounds around you. You may even turn your head side to side or up and down to give you more range of hearing your surroundings. Listen to what Nature is telling you.

Allow yourself to become one with your surroundings. Feeling the earth beneath you, breathing down into that space of calm and allow connection. Feel the air as it moves around you, notice how it is stirring the tiny hairs on your arms. Allow the wind to caress you. Breathe even deeper into your consciousness and visualize your face becoming the form of a deer's face. Feel your ears extend out and away from the side of your face, moving up higher, pivoting as they adjust and listen to your surroundings. Feel your nose lengthening along with your mouth and begin to notice how your breath moves into your nostrils differently.

Now focus on your eyes, becoming larger and your perception depth increased as you can now see both sides of your surroundings without having to adjust your head. For a few more breaths connect with the senses of deer. Really hear, see and smell.

With your senses activated and enhanced you are now ready to return to your natural physical human form. Breathing slow and with intent to move your ears, eyes, mouth and nose back to their original positions and breathe into that space of wholeness as you reconnect with yourself and surroundings.

Before leaving your meditative space, give yourself time to adjust once your eyes are open. It is also a good practice to offer gratitude to the earth for holding you and providing you a safe space to go on this meditative journey and connection with deer.

Journal prompts: please give yourself some time to reflect and write down your experience. What did you like? What didn't you like? Were you able to notice a difference with your senses when you focused new energy into them?

"We can judge the heart of man by his treatment of animals."

IMMANUEL KANT

CERNUNNOS

According to Wikipedia, "Cernunnos is the conventional name given in Celtic studies to depictions of the "horned god" of Celtic polytheism." While I think this is an easy or lacking way of going into detail on such a magnificent being, there is some truth there. I believe Cernunnos to be more than just a "blanket" for many. I believe him to be one primary god with his own unique and defining attributes. There are many "horned gods" and to just lump them all under the blanket of "Cernunnos" in my opinion is a disservice to not only Cernunnos but the other horned gods. With animal work we do however lump each animal into its own blanket category with the knowing that, although similar in species and characteristics, no two are identical. Just like no two snowflakes are identical. Each species of animals breaks down into one singular animal with its own essence, soul and authentic instincts.

Cernunnos as "stag" defined as a male deer is in my opinion a celebration and somewhat icon of divine masculinity. Just as the divine feminine is honored as goddess men too have divine masculine beings honored as gods. The two together create balance and union. However, gender in general is something to question as our souls' essence cannot be fixated, nor should it be identified as either masculine or feminine. I would argue that our soul is of no gender. However, for the purpose of this chapter the focus on Cernunnos as "stag" will be highlighting his divine masculine attributes in the hopes to inspire and active "stag like" confidence in you the reader. Whether that "confidence" is linked to gender is solely based upon you the reader and what your needs are in calling on Cernunnos.

What if as humans we struggle with the concept of a "God Head" a "Supreme Being" someone who is holier than thou and has attributes that are unobtainable? What if though, we saw "God" or felt that godlike energy in animals? Wouldn't this way of thinking help us to understand why the ancient one's carved images of animals on stones? Weren't they in essence seeing animals as gods? If we as a society today shifted perspective towards respecting and honoring animals as gods wouldn't our experience with each other as humans begin to shift as well?

FEELING DEER ENERGY WITH YOUR PHYSICAL FORM

Another way of activating connection with Cernunnos is by doing the above meditation in yoga deer pose. This pose is beneficial for opening up the hips, creating balance between both your masculine (right side) and feminine (left side) of the body and improves digestion.

Step by step deer pose:

- Sit in comfortable butterfly position with the soles of your feet together in front of you.
- Swing one leg behind you.
- Sit in this position for a minimum of three deep breaths or 30–60 seconds.
- Lean back and switch legs and repeat.

While in this pose, be sure to keep your spine tall and your face and upper body relaxed. This is a hip and leg pose. You will be activating your root chakra and sacral chakra in this pose. To assist you in energetically calling upon stag or deer energy, think of all the ways you have denied yourself pleasure and natural instinctual urges. Allow yourself awareness and offer up forgiveness while you move the breath through your body clearing away the residual and creating space for new opportunities. This pose is great for creating a new sense of stability and endurance.

RITUAL CONNECTION WITH THE GOD CERNUNNOS

Create a container or space for this meditation connection. Preferably in a dimly lit room, maybe a green candle lit or scrying mirror filled with water. For this meditation check in with your gut and allow your intuition to be activated. Ask yourself what setting feels right to call upon and connect with this ancient deity?

Altar set up:
Cernunnos is often referred to by many titles such as "Horned God, God of Nature, Horned One, God of Animals, Wild One, Stag God." For altar set up a green altar cloth or cloth with Celtic knot work would suffice. If you are feeling more inclined, you can create a full altar in the center of the space where you will be working with him and place your altar or spell work tools in their appropriate directional spaces. Remember, this is your space and container and the connection you are activating is for you.

Physically preparing for ritual connection:
For this connection, position yourself in either deer pose or crossed legged with arms up in similar fashion, you can also do this pose lying down. Give your physical self time to adjust and disconnect from the worries and stresses of the day. Turn off all cellular and technology devices and rest both mentally and physically.

Always begin with your breath. Inhaling to the count of four and exhaling to the count of four. Repeat at least four times, before settling into your own rhythm. In your mind's eye go back to that physical place in Nature and reconnect. Feel the earth beneath you, the air around you and anchor into a calm meditative state.

When you feel like you are moving deeper into a relaxed mental state bring your focus and awareness onto activation. When working with deities, a very quick and effective way to invite them into your space is to speak their name, either out loud or silently. You can chant his name over and over again. Or you can simply ask him that he join you here in this meditative space in whatever form will be most received. Allow yourself time to welcome him energetically.

INVOCATION TO CERNUNNOS:

"Hail Cernunnos,
Horned One, symbol of rebirth and bringer of balance.
Cernunnos who is wild, free and confident!
Cernunnos who is consort to Earth herself!
Hail Cernunnos King of the Animals
and God of Nature."

Once he has joined you, simply seek to see him in any form he chooses and allow him to see you in your highest form. For when we meditate this space is free from ego and insecurities. You sit here in your true energetic form unbound by limitations. Observe how Cernunnos moves and interacts with you and trust the process of activating connection. Remember there is no right or wrong only this moment. Cernunnos is known as Steward and God of the Animals. When connecting with him, maybe you could inquire to him about how you can better serve animals and Nature as a whole. Is there more that you can be doing? Allow him the opportunity to speak to you and communicate in whichever way he decides. After you have spent time with him, offer him gratitude and slowly come back to your physical space.

Journal prompts: write down your experience with Cernunnos. In what form did he appear to you? How was your interaction?

The key really is to acknowledge that you are setting the intent to call upon a specific deity to gain a deeper understanding of his attributes and how you can apply those in your own life. If you feel inspired to cast a circle, please do so! This is your experience. Make it your own and it will have more impact.

For some, developing a relationship with Cernunnos and any god or goddess can be a challenge. I believe that there is an inner battle with our ego. We are taught things and read things or even hear things from other's perspectives and interactions. It is easy to formulate an opinion on something without ever even experiencing it yourself.

In order to ever formulate your own opinion on anything, you have to disconnect from ego and what you have been taught, and experience it for yourself. The purpose of this book is to help each reader acquire different tools and techniques to have at one's fingertips. Make the connections with each animal, god and your physical body unique and true for you. Some animals you will resonate with more, and others not so much, but the key is to embrace the divinity in all of them.

Yoga philosophy teaches that God or Om is present in all things. All things! When one says "namaste" they are saying the light in me sees the light in you. Or the god in me sees the god in you. By working with yoga poses to activate one's connection with animals, you are saying the "animal in me sees the animal in you". We are all one! All interconnected and all divine!

When calling upon the gods/goddesses you will almost always read in myths and legends that they each have a companion animal or appear as an animal. There is a reason behind this. There is a reason that Cernunnos is depicted as a man with stag antlers upon his head. There is a reason one of the most popular carvings of Cernunnos on the Gundestrup Cauldron (image below) which was found in a bog in Northwestern Denmark in 1891 and dated back to the first century BCE. If you look at the image and how he is sitting you can see yoga to be a universal tool to use when connecting and calling upon not just God within but the animals which are one and the same. Has it ever made you wonder why almost all yoga poses are named after and mimic animals?

CHAPTER TEN

SWAN

MEDICINE AND MAGICK

"TRANSFORMATION THROUGH GRACE"

Swans have been honored and revered in Native American traditions. They are considered harmonious. To the Celts they were transient beings observed for their migratory patterns and their connection to water, reminding us that once again the Celts believed and practiced animism and totemism.

When calling upon swan energy, it's important to dive back into one's childhood and remember the story of the Ugly Duckling written by Hans Christian Andersen back in 1843. Swan medicine is all about transformation through self acceptance. Here you have a story about an ugly duckling that is basically rejected by everyone and in its pain of being turned away, bullied and mistreated, it runs away. After seeking solace with a handful of other animals and even people, the little duckling is still rejected and ends up alone and cold in a cave on a frozen lake. When the lake thaws in the spring, the duckling has grown and wakes to find a flock of beautiful swans swimming. In despair, he thrusts himself at the swans thinking they will finally put him out of his misery but instead they embrace him. When he looks into the water and sees his reflection, he realizes that through the winter he had matured into a magnificent swan. Instead of being rejected, he had finally found his family.

Known as waterfowl, swans are the largest animal in the "duck/goose" family. They have a wingspan of about ten feet. They are well known for being majestic and ethereal birds that are for the most part monogamous.

Swans represent patience, honoring the inner struggle and allowing things to unfold in their own way and on their own time frame. Just like the little duckling, there is a hibernation period, a time to rest and retreat. Once you make it through this period knowing that all life moves in cycles, you emerge reborn, transformed and whole.

If you have ever sat and watched a swan on the water there is a deep sense of calm. They emit such a gentile essence that it's almost angelic. It's been rumored that because of their large size they cannot fly but that is not true. They are one of the largest flying birds and when they move in the air they look like angels. Some animal guides implement that when swan energy comes into your life it is a message from beyond.

As an animal that is known for its dramatic transformation one can easily look at swan as a mirror of being able to truly see oneself with love, compassion and trust in the process and flow of life. Oftentimes we have moments of self loathing, where we compare our physical selves, mental and even emotional selves to those around us, much like the little duckling. There is the saying, "Just like the moon, we go in phases." Swans can teach us to float on the waves of life and rest assured, knowing good things are coming. A transformation is beginning!

Swans are highly intelligent and can recognize distinct features in animals (this includes humans) around them. While not known for being aggressive, during their nesting like most animals they can become quite territorial. If a human or other animal is unkind or has attacked it, they will remember that particular individual and not back down or hold back from attacking. They can also remember humans who have been kind to them and they will formulate a close bond with those individuals.

Swans are rumored to have more feathers than any other bird. The big number is said to be about 24,000 in an adult. Their feathers are designed to not only help the bird to fly but keep dry and float on the water. Keep that in mind if you do stumble upon or are gifted a feather of a swan. What are you intending to fly away from or fly too? Or how can you float above the current situation? Feathers used in magick or spellwork are not uncommon. When you know the animal the particular feather comes from, the individual attributes and essence of that animal will only enhance your intention with your magick, spell or ritual.

Another attribute that makes swans unique is their vertebrae. Swans have 23 while ducks have 16 or less, and geese have anywhere between 17 and 23. This extra length allows swans to forage both on land and underwater. Unlike ducks, swans cannot dive under the water, they rely upon their long neck to obtain food. Energetically, you can apply this length of neck to your own self as a mirror – what are you stretching or sticking your neck out for?

MEDITATION TO CONNECT WITH SWAN

For this meditation it is recommended that you find a body of water. Either a lake, pond, river or your own shower or bathtub.

Begin by bringing your awareness to your breath, once again taking a nice slow deep inhale to the count of four and exhale to the count of four. Continue this pattern while simultaneously allowing your physical body to relax. Focus on your forehead, releasing and relaxing, allowing your eyelids to gently close. Feeling the sensation of relaxation move down your cheeks, to your jaw, your neck, your shoulders, arms, forearms all the way down to your fingertips, becoming heavy as they completely relax and float in the water. Focus on this sensation moving down your chest, allowing each inhale and exhalation of your lungs pushing out any tension in your body and let go of the stresses of the day and bask in the pleasure of simply being able to take time for yourself and physically relax in the healing waters. Feel you center, your stomach and your hips releasing all tension as you adjust into a comfortable sitting position. Allow your legs to become completely relaxed from your hip joints, to your thighs, your knees, ankles all the way down to your toes. Here in this physically relaxed state you are ready to go deeper into your subconscious and activate a powerful energetic connection.

Tapping into your mind's eye, allow yourself to disconnect from what you know to be your natural form and begin to see and feel becoming covered with white feathers, hundreds of thousands of feathers, so thick you can't even feel the water you are sitting in. You are giving yourself permission to energetically morph into the shape of a beautiful white swan.

(Pause)

Feel as your bone structure changes into hollow bones that allow you to float upon the water. With your new bones you need not fear the depth of the water for you are designed to stay on top.

Observe the tiny hair like features of each feather as you become more buoyant in the water. Focusing on the white feathers you begin to notice your neck stretching upward, your gaze of perception changes as you become taller and are able to move your long, graceful neck with more flexibility than ever before. Give yourself a few moments to really look around you, maybe you feel inclined to put your head down into the water or turn it all the way around and quite literally look behind you.

(Pause)

Feel your head becoming smaller and your mouth extending out from your body with a thick beak. Taking a nice deep breath, you realize that you can breathe better than you ever could in your human form. Your lungs receive a full inhale bringing in more oxygen during each breath.

Breathing your awareness into your legs, feel as they become shorter and your feet become the wide, webbed feet of a swan. Feel as you pull your feet backwards through the water, allowing your webbed toes to spread apart and allow yourself to push the water back with slight resistance of the water you begin to paddle. Feeling your feather covered body bob up and down as you paddle and move with ease through the water.

For the next few moments allow yourself to be one with swan. Move in the water, dip, dive or simply float. Here as swan you are not weighed down with worries, you are covered with a thick layer of feathers that protect you from the elements and allow you to do more than just swim in water. You can lift off and fly if you want. If you choose to not fly, stretch your wings out to the side and feel that span of energy, that power of knowing you can take off any time you want and glide upon the air currents. Swan energy is not demanding or forceful so allow yourself to feel the calm, gentle and graceful way that you maneuver here in the water or up in the sky.

Journal Prompts: how did it feel being weightless? What are the things that weigh you down the most in life? How can you utilize swan energy to gain a different perspective and float above?

FEELING SWAN ENERGY WITH YOUR PHYSICAL FORM

Swan pose in yoga is very similar to pigeon pose. Just like there are distinct differences between a pigeon and a swan; there are distinct differences in their yoga poses. For one, when moving into swan pose, it is best if you go slow, gracefully and really focus on elongating your neck and spine. The swan pose is both stimulating and energizing.

Step by step guide to getting into swan pose:

- Begin on all fours, in table pose.
- Slide your right knee forward, being aware of any knee discomfort and adjusting if necessary.
- Turn your foot to face the direction of your opposite arm, this will place your ankle in front of your hip.
- Flex your foot and slide your left leg back behind you as far as you comfortably can.
- Allow your hands to stay comfortably in front of you.
- From here you can lift your chin and head or you can slide your arms out in front of you and allow your upper body to relax into a sleeping swan pose.
- Hold for one to three minutes. Then repeat on the other side.

While participating in the yoga poses for each animal, it can help tremendously if, while you are breathing and holding each asana (pose), you close your eyes and visualize yourself as physically embodying the animal.

Swans have been honored and revered. In Native American traditions they are considered harmonious. In Hindu Mythology they are associated with Brahma and his consort Saraswati. The swan of eternity is said to have laid a cosmic egg, thereby assisting Brahma in creating the cosmos. The Irish believed that swans were the embodied souls of the dead. While the Germans considered swans to be symbols of death and the underworld. To the Celts they are transient being observed for their migratory patterns and their connection to water. Reminding us that, once again, the Celts believed in and practiced animism and totemism.

By allowing oneself connection with swan through Brigid we tap into calm, grace and beauty. An inner beauty. Like Brigid, swans are fairly good natured unless provoked. They are also very loving and loyal. Brigid as midwife watches over babies, mothers, families and lovers. She is like a stern but gentle mother or big sister, who, if provoked, will defend with a vengeance, much like swans.

Swans are well known for being monogamous. During your observation of these majestic birds you most likely will see images of two swans pressing their heads together which brings their long necks into the shape of a heart. This image is a very popular one printed on cards for weddings, valentines and other romantic occasions. Most images of Brigid show her with a flame at her heart. Both are symbols of a powerful love, fueled by passion and loyalty. Brigid is, after all, a Goddess of the Hearth and Home. Naturally she will protect and inspire "heartfelt" connections and unions.

GODDESS BRIGID

Brigit the Victorious, Brighid the Immortal Host, Brighid of the Fairy Folk, Bride of Joy, Mother of Songs and Music, The Lady of the Sea. The flame in the heart of women, Mother of Wisdom, Saint Brigit, the poet, the healer, the midwife. Brigit the blacksmith, the warrior, the Great Triple Goddess. She who muses. Source of inspiration and creative arts.

In folklore, her names mean "fiery arrow, bright arrow, exalted one" or "the bright one." She is sacred in Ireland, Britain (which is a derivation of her name) and Scotland. She is believed to be one of the Tuatha de Danaans; an ancient tribe of the gods in Irish mythology. It is rumored that she is the daughter of The Morrigan and the good god Dagda, also known as the Chief of the Gods.

Brigid is celebrated on her feast day of February 1st, also known as Imbolc. This day also marks the northern departure of the migrating swans.

In honor of Brigid, a goddess so loved she was later sainted; it is quite common for those in devotion to her to make a sacred pilgrimage. This Celtic pilgrimage passes through beautiful Irish landscapes from the Lisnawilly Estate and picturesque villages of County Louth, the lush farmlands of Meath, Donadea Forest Park, Coolree Bog, the Grand Canal, Pollardstown Fen and the Curragh of Kildare. Along the route, glittering like jewels in the earth, lie the sacred sites of the Holy Well, Faughart, Knockbridge Standing Stone, also known as the 'Cuchulainn Stone', the Hill of Slane, the Hill of Tara, Brideswell Kilcock, Brigid's Fire Temple and Holy Wells, Kildare. This alignment of sacred sites reflects the Cygnus (swan) constellation which was prominent in the skies at the time of St Brigid's birth in the 5th Century AD.

Cygnus ('swan') is a large northern constellation also known as the Northern Cross. It lays in the plane of the Milky Way – in fact, the Cygnus constellation marks the beginning of what is known as the Great Rift, Dark Rift or Dark River; a band of dark interstellar dust clouds that appears to split a third of the Milky Way lengthwise in half and which extends from Cygnus through to Sagittarius. In the case where the Milky Way is perceived as the body of a goddess, Cygnus would be roughly where her two legs part – in some sense, perhaps her womb. Where it is the World Tree, it would be situated where its roots begin to split from the trunk. It is interesting to think that in Norse mythology, two swans (from which all other swans are descended) are depicted as swimming upon the lake or pool – the Well of Origin – at the base of the Tree. Since Cygnus is found beside the constellation Lyra, it was said by the Greeks that Cygnus represented Orpheus who was transformed into a swan following his death at the hands of the Maenads and placed in the sky next to his beloved lyre. The Cygnus constellation also resembles a sun-wheel or Brigid's Cross.

http://www.thesoulofbones.com/blog/the-cult-of-the-swan

MEDITATION TO CONNECT WITH BRIGID

Sitting in a comfortable position, focus on your breath. Take a nice deep breath in and exhale it out. Continue to breathe and, as you do, become aware of how your body naturally relaxes on each exhale. Begin taking deeper breaths and feel this relaxation drift over your entire body. Breathe in 2... 3... 4... and out 2... 3... 4... (repeat 3 times), now breathing at your own pace; breathing fully and breathing easily. Trusting that your body and mind will relax more and more as you continue to just breathe.

(Pause)

Now that you are relaxed, in your mind's eye see yourself standing bare footed on damp green grass. Feel the cool moisture under your feet. Stand here just breathing in and out. Feel yourself connect with the earth. As you gaze around you see smooth green covered hills with a clear blue sky. The sun is shining and you feel calm and relaxed. Looking out in the distance you can see a moss -covered stone pathway leading up one of the hills nearby. When you are ready, make your way to the path, moving however fast or slow you choose. When you get to the first stone, you stop and just breathe in the crisp moist air. When you are ready, step onto the moss-covered stone path – it too is somewhat damp and cold. You begin to follow the path of stones up to the top of the hill.

(Pause)

When you reach the top of the hill you see a woman dressed all in white in long flowing red hair, the color of flaming fire. She has her back turned to you – at her feet are hundreds of candles encircling her. She is looking off into the distance. You feel hesitant to approach. Slowly she turns and glances over her shoulder she reaches out her left hand motioning for you to approach.

As you slowly and with great humility approach her, you find yourself standing inside the circle of candles, your shoulder almost touching hers.

She smiles at you and places her arm around you bringing you in closer. She doesn't speak and she doesn't have to. You know who she is. You know her strength – you can feel it. She is the Celtic Goddess Brigid – the keeper of the sacred fire and healing waters.

You stand there with your arms embracing one another, hip to hip, side by side gazing out into the distance. What you are gazing at is your future – it will appear as you see you it.

(Pause)

It may appear as many roads, many hills, many opportunities. It is yours to see and yours to understand.

She moves you to face her and she smiles again at you. Not a big grin but a calm, loving, motherly smile, reassuring you that you are strong and capable. She kisses you on the forehead, your intuitive eye, and you feel an electric spark where her lips touched you. This is her way of igniting your intuition. Next, she moves her hand to your heart. This is her way of lighting a fire inside you. She is the Keeper of the Sacred Flame and she has placed that flame's spark into your heart space. Activating you. Empowering you. Filling you up with warm confidence.

Next, she takes both of your hands into hers and just holds them. She speaks but her message is for you and you alone.

(Pause)

When her message is heard she releases your hands and motions for you to return back to the stone pathway. Before you leave, however, she bends down and picks up one of the candles encircling you both and places it in your hands. You notice as you leave that you are dressed all in white, still barefooted. You feel calm, reassured and awakened in your purpose and inspired to create. With your candle in your hands you turn and give thanks to the Goddess Brigid for her mystery and sacred healing. You feel reborn. As you slowly move back down the moss-covered stone pathway, you are calm and confident. You have a hunger inside your belly – but it is not for food. Take a few breaths here – What are you craving? What will satisfy you? What will fill you up?

(Pause)

See yourself at the bottom of the hill, back where you started. Feel once more the damp green grass under your feet. Breathe in the fresh crisp air. With each inhale making you more aware of your surroundings. With each exhale you begin to move your hands and feet. Slowly coming back to the present.

Journal Prompts: What did your future look like? Did she have a particular message for you? What are you craving? What is going to fill you up?

RITUAL CONNECTION WITH BRIGID AS SWAN

For this particular ritual you will need either a large glass bowl or cauldron and a vial.
This ritual is focused on creating Sacred Holy Water to use in healing rituals, elixirs and other spellwork.

Altar Prep: white cloth, white candles, vials or chalices of water, sun wheels or Brigid's crosses.

Stones that are commonly used when working with Brigid: citrine, golden calcite, yellow fluorite, carnelian.

Sacred herbs: hawthorn, oak, nettle, mistletoe, cowslip, fennel, flax, shamrock, mugwort, rue, lemon peels, fresh or dried orange slices (these represent sunshine).

Images or figurines: swans and/or statues of Brigid or swan feathers.

Set up your altar in your own way. Leaving in the center a space large enough for your bowl or cauldron. Call in the directions, cast a circle and create your container for spell work as you normally would do.

Once you have created your magickal space, it is time to begin. Slowly and with intent pour your water from your vials or chalices into the bowl or cauldron, asking Brigid to bless the water as it is poured. Next add your chosen stones and herbs. Allow yourself time to sit and breath into the space. Here in this space allow your eyes to rest and focus on your breathing. Give yourself time to feel the energy around you and go into a meditative space. See yourself sitting on a very green patch of grass.

In your mind's eye, picture your bowl or chalice as a perfectly round lake. You may see ripples and the light shimmering as you intensify your focus. Floating on the water you see the most elegant, white swan. The swan is simply paddling its webbed feet in this crystal clear lake, almost as if it is stirring the sacred waters you have created with herbs and stones. There is a deep love that emanates from this swan's eyes as it gazes down into the water. The swan begins to gently move into a circle, rotating over and over again. The water is being stirred in a circular pattern. The swan suddenly stops and plunges its head down into the depths of the water and pulls out a stone. Holding the stone in its mouth, it swims to the edge of the lake where you are sitting on your patch of grass. It leaves the water and approaches you, dropping the stone at your feet. Allow your eyes to gently open as you adjust back into your physical surroundings.

You may sit at your altar or kneel. You may place your hands in the water and begin to stir; you may even use your swan feather. If you have one to stir with, place it inside the bowl or cauldron. After you have placed your hands into the water, you may take them out and anoint the top of your head, forehead, throat and heart. If you are familiar with the Chakras, you may anoint them as well. Place upon your body the water blessed by swan and Brigid. When you are ready, reach into the depth and pull out a stone. Is it the same stone?

As we say goodbye for the time being to the Celtic gods and goddesses and their animal counterparts and journey into the north, let's look back at some quick reminders. If you are feeling stuck emotionally or spiritually, you can call upon the energy of raven to help you rise up above and look at things with a new perspective. A quick and easy way is to go into your meditative state and activate raven through shapeshifting and see below you the obstacles you are facing or the things that are blocking your direction. By activating raven energy, you will be able to focus free from ego and see what needs to be done rather than only seeing what is right before you. You can also call upon horse energy to help you break free, run wild or, if necessary, stay where you are with determination and strength.

Remember that we are usually the ones that put obstacles in our own paths. We are the worst at self sabotaging our progress. Activate your guttural instincts and remember you are an animal. So act like one! If you are feeling weighed down and hopeless why not shapeshift with swan and float for a bit? Does the situation at hand absolutely need to be dealt with right this minute? Or can you sit in a warm bath, close your eyes and be swan simply bobbing on the water. You can also call upon deer energy to help you tap into your senses. Maybe the solution has already presented itself but you were not really listening. Most people listen to respond not to actually hear. Deer energy will give you that reminder that you must use your ears – hear what is being said and see what is happening around you.

Another great way to work through any situation at hand with the assistance of animals is to go into ritual space. I'm reminded of when my dear friend and colleague Courtney Weber Hoover came to Utah to co-host an all-day Celtic magick event that was focused on shapeshifting and the attributes of The Morrigan. Courtney took us into The Morrigan's cave and together she and I helped each guest through ritual meditation to shapeshift into an animal or other aspect of The Morrigan.

By entering a dark space, letting go of all the things that one claims as identifying factors such as one's name, gender, relationships, family, home, job, religion and ideals; each guest was simply there, beings of energy ready and willing to embrace what was being offered in the dark of her cave. Once the shift occurred, Courtney and I walked around with a mirror and offered encouragement as each guest saw what they had shifted into. It was a very powerful and moving ritual.

When you allow yourself to disconnect from ego brain and simply be in a state of receptivity, the doors to possibilities open. When you allow yourself to disconnect from old ways of thinking that animals are lesser species and property to own you realize that, as mammals also, we have created a disconnect with the greatest masters and teachers of all time. Animals have survived since the very beginning and they continue to adapt and evolve. Can we? The Ancient Celts believed this. They left behind carved images that clearly showed their love and respect for their animal kin, even their personal names and clan names imply that they were descended from animals. For example, the name Brannogenos means "son of the raven" and Cunogenos means "son of the dog".

The surface of Celtic animals and their counterpart deities has only been scratched. If the Celts call to you; study, observe and research. There is so much more to learn and so many more animals to connect with. What a gift to have amongst us these sentient, divine beings – wholes unto themselves and with so much knowledge to give, if we only humble ourselves to see it and receive it with gratitude.

Nordic Animals as Gods

CHAPTER ELEVEN

HONEY BEE

MEDICINE AND MAGICK

"The busy bee has no time for sorrow."

WILLIAM BLAKE

The very first bees evolved from wasps about 150 million years ago in the era known as the Cretaceous. About 20 million years ago bees, particularly bumblebees, journeyed from Siberia to North America. Here they thrived and spread. Currently there are about 25,000 known species of bee with about 250 known from the UK.

Bees are in the order Hymenoptera which means "veil-winged" family and includes ants and wasps, from which bees evolved. The Hymenoptera is just one of many orders of insects on the planet making up about 70% of all known species on Earth. However, this number is drastically dropping as humans have essentially taken over the planet. History has shown that with mankind comes destruction, whether by hunting to extinction or driven to extinction because their prey and habitats disappearing. It is estimated that one species goes extinct every twenty minutes. Out of this number, only three bumblebee species have gone extinct globally but with more to follow.

Insects are responsible for delivering numerous 'ecosystem services' such as pollination and decomposition, and there is no doubt that little life on Earth (including ourselves) could survive without them. As the famous biologist E. O. Wilson said, *'If all mankind were to disappear, the world would regenerate back to the rich state of equilibrium that existed ten thousand years ago. If insects were to vanish, the environment would collapse into chaos."*

Honey bees represent productivity, hard work, community and staying focused on the task at hand. They are very service and goal oriented. Some would say that bees are the inspiration for creating unity within communities. They have a unique and highly effective way of communicating with each other in their colony. Honey bee colonies consist of one queen, hundreds of male drones and anywhere between 20,000 to 80,000 female worker bees. Within this colony there are specific roles and jobs each individual must meet. It takes everyone working together and fulfilling their specific roles to create a thriving colony.

History has shown that humans of the past valued bees. The Druids saw bees as images of the Sun Goddess and cause for celebration and bringing the community together. In Aegean the bee was seen as the bridge between this world and the underworld. Monks lived in huts shaped like beehives, which represented the goal of community balance. According to German lore, bees came to Earth from the underground paradise where they lived as the fates. In Norse legend, the tears of the goddess Freya were said to be made of bee's gold. In India bees are symbol of the Goddess of the Moon.

The Greeks looked to bees as a mirror of society. The Minoans saw bees as symbols of Goddess Potnia which in Greek means "Mistress, Lady, Goddess."

Seen as a demi-god or King of Crete, "Melisseus" was known for being one of the first to offer sacrifice to the gods and to formally introduce rites and religious processions. He had two daughters, Amalthaea and Melissa, who nourished the infant Jupiter with goat's milk and honey. Hence arose the poets' tale that bees flew up and filled the child's mouth with honey. Melissa, by her father, was made first priestess of the Magna Mater; and from this fact the representatives of the goddess are still termed Melissae. Those who served as Priestesses of the Goddess were titled "Melissae" which means "bee". We are seeing a resurgence in the term "Melissae" as goddess-centered communities are beginning to rapidly expand, those who are in service as priestesses are now once again being referred to as "Melissae". The Pythian pre-olympic Priestess of Delphi was named "The Delphic Bee." In fact, the second temple to be built at Delphi was rumored to have been built by bees.

The list can and does go on and on when it comes to bees being revered and honored as ethereal, divine and godlike. Additional resources and links have been provided.

When one sits and observes bees, for the sake of this book, bumblebees or the ones we typically know to make honey, specifically the *apis mellifera* which is Latin for "bee" and *mellifera*, Latin for "honey baring"; there are some key things to pay attention to. Firs, can you see how they all work together? There is a camaraderie amongst the bees that is quite inspiring. How often do you see this behavior in our modern day world?

One bee colony is capable of producing 60–100 pounds of honey per year. That is quite a team or family effort. When we look at honey bees as mirrors of what our possibilities are as humans living in this world, it's vital to pay attention to how we communicate. Bees have a language of their own. They communicate to each other. This is an absolute must in order for their colonies to survive. When communicating, bees use movement, odor cues or pheromones. The use of pheromones is the "Queens job". She is the one who sends out pheromones to keep female worker bees interested in work, not mating. The queen bee will also send out pheromones when she wants to invite drone bees (males) to mate with her. Have you ever been stung by a bee? If you have, you will know that, once stung, more bees will swarm to defend their own.

When looking to bees for inspiration, it is vital to take the time to analyze your own communication skills. Do you ask for help when you need it? Are you giving clear instructions or detailed information when you do ask for help? Being specific in how one speaks to others is pivotal in living in a community as a fully engaged member. Be clear and precise. Otherwise there are bound to be miscommunications that create their own domino effect of mishaps which could have been prevented with clear, concise communication. A big key in having good communication is knowing what you want. Can you be the "queen" of your own life and delegate? Bee energy is all about being focused on who you are in your colony, being fully present, aware and conscious. Bees survive as a whole because they work together. Do we as humans value our survival enough to work together?

Albert Einstein said, "If the bee disappeared off the surface of the globe then man would only have four years of life left. No more bees, no more pollination, no more plants, no more animals, no more man." Over one third of our food supply relies upon bees for their pollination skills. Pollination is vital for the reproduction of the plants. For example, honey bees are major pollinators for apples, blueberries, cantaloupes, cherries, cucumbers, sunflowers, watermelon, avocados, peaches, nectarines, rose hips, alfalfa, strawberries, apricots, broccoli, cabbage, cauliflower, grapes, cocoa, clover and tomatoes; just to name a few.

Now more than ever, we really need to step up as a society and do our part to help bees survive so that our future posterity can have a future. We are seeing a drastic decline in honey bees due to insecticides, herbicides and habitat loss. With hand-pollination on a large scale being near impossible (and also expensive), without bees our access to fresh fruits and vegetables would decline tremendously. Currently, as of August 2018, there are eight species of bees on the endangered list.

So what are some ways you can physically attract bees and help them survive as a fellow member of our human communities? We really need to all band together and do our part to ensure bees survive so that we can survive. Here are some simple tips:

- Plant flowers that attract bees (wildflowers).
- Plant single petal flowers as these produce more pollen (foxglove, asters, clover, roses, zinnias, etc).
- Plant yellow, blue, purple and white flowers as these colors attract bees more than reds, oranges and pinks.
- Plant flowering vegetables and fruits.
- Plant herbs that attract bees (mint, lavender, rosemary, sage, thyme, borage, cilantro, etc).
- Provide a bee shelter / insect "hotel".
- Stop using pesticides.....Please!

https://www.wikihow.com/Attract-Honey-Bees

THE POWER OF HONEY – ELIXIR OF GOLD

Another one of bees' messages is to enjoy the "sweet" things in life. We all have days, weeks, months and occasionally years where everything seems to be falling apart or in actuality falling into place. Bees make honey – this sweet, golden elixir.

Honey is antiviral, antiseptic, anti-fungal, anti-inflammatory and anti-bacterial. Honey is an excellent source of antioxidants which protect your body from free radicals. It also has an incredible shelf life. If preserved properly, there really is no expiration date. Honey has been found in the pyramids by archaeologists which dates back 3000 years. These pots of honey were not spoiled! The ancient people saw bees as "magical" because of their ability to make honey. The Egyptians used honey as we use bandaids today, to cover, protect and help heal wounds. Honey was used as an embalming agent. It has been left as offerings to the gods. Aphrodite, Goddess of Love and Beauty, would be a sacred goddess to offer honey to as a libation. The Ancient Hindu texts discuss honey as being one of five elixirs for immortality.

In magic and spellwork, honey is an ingredient that most solitary practitioners have used or will use in their witchcraft. Honey is sticky, so for binding spells, unions and marriages it can be quite effective. If you are wanting to bring more sweetness into your life, honey will be a good addition to your intention. Those who do kitchen magic, hedge witchery, Hoodoo, folk magick or herbal healing will definitely want to use honey. Please make sure that you are supporting your local community and bee colony by purchasing local honey. The product you find in the store has been heated, processed and chemically altered.

To bring sweetness into your life and also stimulate your immune system, you can take fresh garden sage, chop it fine, place it in a jar and cover it with honey. You can also do this with fresh garlic to make a very potent and powerful antibacterial remedy. Please see Susun Weed's Youtube channel for more recipes:

https://youtu.be/ub7URpF6UZI

THE POWER OF BREATH WORK AND YOUR VOICE

In part one we utilized yoga poses to help activate our connection with animals. In part two we will add the power of sound and breath work. If you have ever attended a public ritual or ceremony, you have most likely participated in humming, singing or chanting. Humming is highly beneficial for your physical body as it reduces stress, promotes a calm soothing vibration, helps to lower heart rate and blood pressure and it increases oxytocin – the hormone that makes us happy! Have you ever buzzed?

The sound that we as humans hear as buzzing from bees is actually the sound their wings make by beating so fast. The larger the bee, the slower its wings beat, so its buzz will sound different. Bees beat their wings (not flap like a bird) about 200–230Hz (cycles per second). That's a lot! Buzzing like humming shifts our mental status from a distracted conscious brain to a focused, present moment brain allowing us to align our subconscious with our conscious and enter a meditative state and focus easier. Have you ever attempted to let your mind wander while humming? It will be very difficult. Humming and buzzing are both ways to stay present during ritual and disconnect from ego brain.

For the next 30 seconds, hum nice and low. Open your mouth slightly and place your tongue behind your teeth. Hum until you feel the vibration at the top of your head.

Now try buzzing for 30 seconds. Pick the one that resonates with you the most and then repeat three more times for 30 second intervals.

Journal Prompts: what did you notice within when you were buzzing and/ or humming?

There really isn't a yoga pose for the bumblebee. However, there is a breathing technique that has been used by the ancient yogis to assist one in activating the crown and heart chakra. The breath work is called "Bhramari Pranayama" which means bumblebee breath. This type of breath work helps increase energy and ward off anxiety.

Step by Step Guide:

- Sitting in a comfortable cross legged position, relax your shoulders.
- Close your throat so you can hear your breath when you breathe in.
- Cover your ears with your thumbs and your eyes with your fingers.
- Inhale through both nostrils and exhale slowly, creating a sound like a bee with the mouth closed. It sounds more like a Mmmmmm than a Bzzzzzzzz.

https://www.yogajournal.com/practice/buzz-away-the-buzzing-mind

MEDITATION TO CONNECT WITH BUMBLE BEE

Sitting in a comfortable position, allow your eyes to gently close and bring your awareness to your breath. Take a nice deep inhale to the count of four and exhale to the count of four. Repeat this breathing technique until you feel your entire physical body and mind enter a peaceful state.

In your mind's eye, visualize yourself in a garden filled with the most colorful wildflowers. It is a hot summer's day and the flowers seem to be dancing in the breeze. Give yourself permission to see all the different colors, you may even begin to smell their sweet fragrance. Here in this garden you begin to hear quite a bit of humming. As you lean down to take a closer look at the flowers you see there are bees moving from flower to flower, their buzzing almost creates a melody and song as they continue about with their work of pollinating.

Sitting here in this garden, you are ready to activate bee energy. So you begin to buzz, allowing your buzz to match that of the bees around you. The more you buzz, the smaller your physical form becomes and you find yourself shifting into the form of a bee. You feel your tiny wings beating fast and you acknowledge that the buzz really is coming from your wings beating at such a rapid pace. Allowing your throat to rest, you breathe into this buzz coming from your body. Gazing around the garden at this size you see how immense and colorful everything is, each flower petal seems to change color to ultraviolet. The shinier the flower, the more the pollen.

Feeling physically light, you listen to the beating of the other bees and they seem to be telling you which flowers to gather from. There are hundreds of bees all around the garden now; buzzing and happy, working together to gather as much pollen as possible. Allow yourself to connect and embrace with the colony as one of its members. This is a group effort and everyone is happy to help out for the greater good.

(Pause)

Now that you have felt the energy and camaraderie of bee life, it is time to bring your awareness back to your own buzz. Through your mouth you begin to buzz, which allows you to once again shift into your human form. Feel your body become large as your physical buzz becomes louder. When you are ready, open your eyes and gently pat your body activating connection with your physical form once more.

Journal Prompt: How did you feel as bee? How would the modern world shift if people became more community oriented and worked together? Do you embrace service work and if so what have you learned as bee that would help you and your community as a whole?

GODDESS BEYLA

In all actuality, there is very little if any evidence in historical writings that would suggest the early Nordic people honored a goddess by the name of Beyla as Goddess of Bees. Beyla is known to be Byggvir's wife and the Goddess Freya and Freyr's servant. Freya is known in legend to weep tears of amber and her very essence contains honey. Naturally, Beyla would be there with Freya to support this theory. However, I choose to believe that now more than ever we need to embrace a goddess devoted to bees and, for me personally, I choose Beyla.

Beyla is linked to land. Her name in Old Norse means "Little Bean." Some say she is the personification of manure, which plants need to thrive. I challenge you the reader to formulate your own opinion. In the Poetic Edda "Lokasenna", Beyla and her husband are mentioned briefly as attendees of the banquet of the god's. It is at this feast that Beyla exchanges insults with Loki who just insulted the Goddess Sif. In my opinion, leave it to true "Queen Bee" to stand up for her own.

BEYLA: "The mountains shake,
and surely I think
From his home comes Hlórriði now;
He will silence the man
who is slandering here
Together both gods and men."

LOKI: "Be silent, Beyla!
thou art Byggvir's wife,
And deep art thou steeped in sin;
A greater shame
to the gods came ne'er,
Befouled thou art with thy filth."

Because of the lack of written evidence, one can look to Beyla's husband for insight on their combined attributes. Byggvir is NOT a god. He is husband, servant and maid to Freya. Together, however, Beyla and Byggvir are the embodiments of agriculture and forestry. Bygg means barley. Byggvir also exchanged insults with Loki at the Feast of the God's mentioned in the "Lokasenna."

It's interesting that supposed servants would be able to address, defend and insult Loki in the presence of the gods if they themselves were not well respected in the company of gods.

With bees in danger of extinction and humans soon to follow, the time is now to shift one's perspective and call to any god or goddess in the hopes of attracting planetary healing for bees. As a rumored Goddess of the Earth and Agriculture, maybe it's time to reconnect with her as an ally in order to save humanity from demise. After all, this Earth, this goddess that we stand upon will outlive us all. She doesn't need us! But we need her and our future posterity needs her and if we can't do our part to save the bees, who will?

MEDITATION TO CONNECT WITH BEYLA

Begin once more with your breath. Allowing yourself a space that is quiet and free from distraction. Really focus on your intent which is to connect with your ideal of the Bee Goddess. Move the wave of your inhale and exhale into a meditative rhythm; inhaling to the count of four and exhaling to the count of four. Repeat this pattern as you consciously move through your physical body from forehead to feet allowing all tension to release and giving your physical body time to relax.

(Pause)

In this state of deep relaxation you are ready to go within into your mind's eye which you imagination is fluid, limitless and free. Allow yourself once more the opportunity to become small, much smaller than you are now. You are a tiny bee once more and here you are inside the hive of your colony. You have journeyed into the hive after a day of gathering pollen and you have come to speak to the Queen Bee or Queen Mother of the colony.

As you move through the hive and the vibration of other bees buzzing, you can smell the wax and the sweetness of honey. At times the aroma can be overwhelmingly intoxicating. You are not working inside the hive at this moment but searching through the combs for the queen who is busy laying eggs.

Once you locate the queen, you ask for only a few moments of her time. Queen's are busy, they have a job to do and that is to ensure the survival of the colony. As you fly past the bees who are her protectors, she observes your entry into her domain and offers a pause of acknowledgement.

As you hover in front of her you come filled with questions. Questions you have always wanted to ask someone who is wise, and determined to help others survive.

You may come before the queen hungry for community, a tribe, a family that accepts you as you are. You may come before the queen ready for more responsibility within your current family, community or tribe. Your reason for seeking the queen today is yours and yours alone. Anytime you come before the gods, you do so with solitary intentional purpose. What is your intent with connecting with Beyla? Give yourself a few moments to really connect with Beyla, in whatever form you see her as or feel to be hers, know that it is right and correct for you. After all, this is your meditative space and only you can dictate how you will perceive her.

In these next few moments give yourself over to asking questions. Seeking guidance and allow yourself time to hear, really hear, absorb and receive. For no matter how busy the bee, they always make time for family and you are kin with the Bee Goddess Beyla.

(Pause)

Once you have spent time with the Queen Bee, you are ready to leave. You offer gratitude and, as you begin to fly out of the entrance of the hive, you bring your awareness back to your breath and with each inhale and exhale you return more and more to your human form. Taking with you the answers to the questions you asked the Queen Bee Beyla.

Journal Prompts: take a few moments and journal your experience. What did the hive look like? What was the energy like inside as all the bees were working so hard to fulfill their roles and responsibilities for the day? How was your interaction with the queen once you found her? Did she offer you council like a mother would? Is her council and advice something you can offer and bring into your own community?

MEAD-ELIXIR OF THE GODS

Together as Byggvir of barley and Beyla of bees, one can come to the conclusion that these two were crafters of mead, also known as the elixir of the gods or nectar of the gods. Mead originated from the African continent over 20,000 years ago.

What is mead? Basically, mead is fermented honey infused with fruit or herbs. It is believed to be the first fermented beverage. While there are many, many types and varieties of mead, it is considered to be a very sacred and honored drink, typically utilized in rituals, ceremonies and weddings. The sweeter the mead, the sweeter the marriage.

Mead was believed to bestow virility by the Greeks. The Anglo-Saxons drank it to induce creativity. It is said that Odin gained his strength by drinking mead, interestingly mead from a goat!? After battle, maidens would reward the warriors who returned with mead. Mead was also consumed as a health remedy.

Mead consists of three main ingredients: honey, water and yeast. Depending on where you live and what season you are experiencing, you can add fresh herbs and fruits to add healing powers and different flavors to your mead. The art of making mead can be a form of devotion in itself. To honor the power of honey with your mead making is to honor the bees and Earth Goddess.

For additional information and recipes:

https://www.mybeeline.co/en/p/what-is-mead-the-drink-of-the-gods

LIFE OF THE QUEEN BEE

"When a queen bee first hatches, she is known as a virgin queen. One of her first priorities upon emerging is to eliminate the presence of other queens. This process usually involves the killing of an existing queen and/or additional queen larvae. Six days after emerging, the virgin queen will leave the hive on a mating flight on which she will mate with up to 20 drones. When the queen's sperm sac, or spermatheca, is full she returns to the colony. Once having mated, the queen will never leave the colony again, unless in the case of swarming. Three days after mating, the queen will begin to lay up to 1000 eggs a day for the rest of her life. Queen bees, on average, have a lifespan of two to five years and can lay around 200,000 eggs a year. Queen rearing is a process brought about by the worker bees to produce a new queen. When a hive is preparing to swarm, has a queen preforming at a substandard level, or when a queen is lost or dies, the worker bees will begin construction of new queen cells to host a queen, or will adjust the diet of a worker larva to produce a new queen."

http://blogs.evergreen.edu/terroir-zack/life-cycle-of-the-honey-bee/

If you were to use the "Queen Bee" archetype as a mirror, what is your kingdom like? What is your primary goal in this kingdom? Are you willing to fight for it? Can you see your primary goal so clearly that you are willing to dedicate yourself to it each and every day?

A queen bee kills the current queen so that she can rule the colony. Then she devotes her entire existence to laying eggs and ultimately birthing the colony and ensuring its survival. Would you be willing to devote every breath, every minute to your community's survival?

RITUAL TO CONNECT WITH BEYLA IN HONOR OF BEES

This ritual can be done indoors or out if you have a garden plot ready to prep.

Altar set up:
Yellow, gold or beehive patterned cloth. Yellow or gold candles. Bowl of water. Bee attracting flower seed packets. Small dish or pot to start your seeds in, along with some dirt and water.

Chalice and mead. Honey and your favorite chocolate bar. Image of a bee or Beyla.

Ritual intent:
In this ritual you will be calling upon Beyla to assist you in healing your connection to bees and asking her for advice and input on how to better serve bees so that our civilization can remain intact.

Begin by creating space, container, casting your circle:
Do this in your own way. Whether you are doing this ritual solitary or with a Coven or Grove, it is important you honor your traditions and those who birthed those traditions. Once your container, circle or space is created it's time to call in the goddess.

In preparation for calling in the Bee Goddess:
Do so by either standing or sitting before your altar. You can close your eyes or focus on the image you have in the center of your altar. Go into your Bhramari Pranayama breath or you can simply buzz. If you choose to buzz, allow yourself time to disconnect form being silly and step out of ego brain, letting your body physically feel the buzz more through you.

Call to Beyla:
Once you have felt the energy rise and shift. it's time to invite the goddess. While there are numerous ways to invite a deity, this ritual is yours, so making it unique to you is key. In my rituals we have called in deities with long and lengthy invocations, song or my personal favorite; chanting the deity name over and over again. Beginning as a whisper then getting louder to back to a whisper.

"Great Goddess Beyla, Lady of Bees.
She who encourages us to work together as a community
to ensure our own survival.
We call to you as one of your own

buzzing and ready to do our part.
We call to you Beyla, Beyla, Beyla!
Hail and Welcome."

Light your candle and pour your mead into your chalice as a libation to the goddess. Begin to pour your dirt into your pot with the intent to impregnate the earth with sacred seed that will grow, flourish and nourish the bees. Once you have placed some dirt into the pot you can add a couple of drops of mead followed by more dirt and then pick up your seeds, ask the Goddess Beyla to bless them that they will grow and attract bees. Place your seeds into the pot and tuck them in with more dirt. Then lightly sprinkle them with water.

Give thanks to the Goddess for helping you with this intention to honor her and serve *ALL* by creating a sanctuary for bees in your yard. In celebration, take your chocolate and dip it into the honey, taking a bite and allowing yourself to savor the sweetness and beauty of living life devoted to the survival of *all* – for animals, plants and humankind need bees in order to survive.

Open the container:
Offer your gratitude to the goddess and open your container, circle or space in your own way. Nurture and care for you seeds, give them plenty of sunshine and, once large enough, transplant them into your garden.

PLANTS THAT ATTRACT HONEY BEES

The best way to connect with bee energy is to create a space or sanctuary for bees. This will give you plenty of opportunities to observe them and begin to appreciate them more. If you are able, you can also research owning a beehive or make arrangements to visit a local apiary and meet with the beekeeper. The best way to learn anything is to find a master and be humble enough to be taught.

When planting in your own garden, make sure to research which plants will grow best in your particular zone and then study the plants to become aware of their individual needs. Remember to NOT spray your yard with pesticides! "The art of gardening is not only a form of relaxation, but also of creating change."

hyssop	goldenrod	zinnia
aster	echinacea	marigolds
basil	dandelions	chives
black eyed Susan	pansies	mint
lilac	pussy willow	sage
clover	snowdrops	nasturtium
cotoneaster	peony	thyme
currant	milkweed	oregano
elderberry	bee balm	
lavender	phlox	

https://thehoneybeeconservancy.org/2017/03/27/21-flowers-that-attract-bees/

www.beesponsible.com/save-the-bees

CHAPTER TWELVE

HAWK

MEDICINE AND MAGICK

"Intelligence without ambition is like a bird without wings."

SALVADOR DALI

Whether you are intentionally seeking to connect with hawk or you are curious as to why hawk has been reaching out to you; gaining a basic knowledge or background of hawk can be vital in your searching or quest for answers and direction.

Hawks are very regal and stunning birds. They have been worshipped, honored and respected as messengers and guides in almost every culture, pantheon, tribe or clan. It's no wonder most people stop and admire a hawk when they see one. They are incredibly beautiful and, whether small or large, they captivate us.

Hawks are natural predators in the "Accipitridae" family of small to large, carnivorous birds. They have distinct sharp hooked bills and feed on smaller prey, anything from insects to small to medium sized mammals.

Hawks are unusual because the female hawk is much larger than the male. In some cases almost twice the size of the males. Hawks have quite the elaborate mating ritual. The male dives in attack mode at the female who is in flight, she in return rolls in the air, presenting her claws. They continue to dive and screech at each other in the air in a circular motion. They will repeat this mating dance until the male finally latches onto the female where they both freefall down towards the ground. It's a very intense and passionate mating ceremony.

Hawks mate for life and are very attached to their nesting territory. Their nests are made high up in the trees and are fairly large in size. The mated pair will use the same nest for many years, adding to it more branches, moss and twigs during nesting season. Hawks will ferociously defend their nesting territory against all predators. The female usually lays two to five eggs and incubates them alone or with her mate. Hawk parents are very watchful and protective of their young.

Richard Donner's film *Ladyhawke*, released in 1984, is about two lovers who have been cursed by the evil bishop. *Isabeau* (played by Michelle Pfeiffer) is forced to spend her days as a hawk cared for by *Navarre* (played by Rutger Hauer) who is a falconer, and his curse is to care for her as hawk by day and then he lives as a wolf by night and she does her best to protect him from hunters at night.

There is a scene where *The Mouse* (played by Matthew Broderick) devises a plan to dig a hole which would allow the two lovers to escape the dawn, which transforms them both, and they could connect in human form once more and realize their love. It is such a beautiful scene and tragic as the sun hits them both in human form and she is once more shifted into a hawk. The piercing cry of her screaming out as a hawk is so painfully heartbreaking.

This movie really shows the power of animal shapeshifting and the connection between animal and human as really not being so separate as we have been taught to believe. Whether we have paid attention to really see it or not, we are really not that different from animals. What separates us really is our mindset. Just like what separates the spirit realm from the physical could simply just be our perspective.

When you google "hawk messages" or "hawk medicine" the most common attribute you will come upon is perspective. Bird medicine is just that perspective. The ability to rise above and see things with new eyes or be able to turn and take in new insight on what it is you are really seeing, if you are really seeing in the first place.

Hawks are known for their keen eyesight. They can spot the tiniest mouse in a field and without warning do a surprise attack so quick the mouse was most likely unaware it was even being hunted. Think of the saying "hawk eye" or "eyes like a hawk." The ability to see what most would not be able to is one of the key attributes of hawk medicine. They are observant, watching, studying and hunting their prey until just the right moment. They are perfect mirrors, teachers and messengers of embracing focused intent and seeing with a new depth.

FALCONRY

Falconry is a style of hunting wild animals by means of a trained bird of prey such as a falcon, hawk or eagle. Most often, in modern falconry, a red tailed hawk is utilized. The art of falconry is said to have begun in Mesopotamia around 2000 BC. Falconry was most likely brought to Europe somewhere around 400 AD when the Huns and Alans invaded from the East.

Falconry was said to be a sport made popular among the nobles of medieval Europe, the Middle East and the Mongolian Empire. Falconry began to lose its popularity around the 17th century once firearms came into play as a more assessable and easier tool for hunting.

There is a deep love, trust and respect between falconer and hawk. The bird completely trusts the falconer to not steal its food and to provide it with protection, and the falconer trusts the bird to come back. Of course their relationship doesn't start out too mutually respectful. The birds are trapped and then trained to work with the falconers. It takes great discipline and one must be taught first through a mentorship with a Master Falconer before going off on their own.

This is a talent. Not everyone can be a falconer. It can take weeks to find a hawk that is right for trapping, not to mention there are only specific birds that are allowed to be trapped for this purpose, and then training can take much longer. Not to mention the falconer has to formulate a bond with a wild bird that has been taken out of its natural habitat. I am assuming that there may be some hesitation and resistance involved. Or there could be complete gratitude now that they are safe from larger predatory birds and are being housed and fed. It really is all one's perspective, which is why working with birds as messengers and guides is such a powerful tool.

Why go to all the trouble to be trained by a master, spend months trapping, training and then, after a couple of hunting seasons, the bird is eventually released back into the wild? Maybe this is still a respected form of devotion to Nature and a working relationship that brings new life to ancient hunting practices. After all, just about anyone can go and get a license to buy a gun. There is something beautiful about taking time and dedication to be trained to work side by side with a wild animal as partners who are devoted to each other.

HAWKS IN MYTHS AND LEGENDS

The Egytian God Horus is associated with hawks. A hawk was linked to the soul and according to historians "a hawk was often released at the time of internment to illustrate the flight of the soul through the realms of the afterlife." Hawk was a royal bird.

The Valkyries who were entrusted to bring the fallen warriors to Valhalla according to Norse mythology were said to shapeshift into hawks.

Apollo, another sun god, had a hawk as a companion and together they were believed to have powers of protection. Apollo worked side by side with the hawk as a messenger from the gods.

North American Natives believed that the hawk embodied the souls of their ancestors. The warriors believed that by calling upon hawks as teachers they would be better warriors and were receiving assistance from an ancestor in the form of hawk.

Going back to Norse mythology, at the very top branch of Yggdrasil there sits an eagle. On the beak of that eagle sits a hawk named Vedrfolnir, in Old

Norse this means "storm pale, wind bleached" or "wind withered." While the reason behind the hawk sitting between the eagle's eyes is not clear, as we do not have access to those who first told the tales of Yggrdasil, one can still speculate. John Lindow has guessed that "the hawk must be associated with the wisdom of the eagle and that perhaps, like Odin's ravens, it flies off acquiring and bringing back knowledge."

MEDITATION TO CONNECT WITH HAWK

Once again, go into your meditative state by taking notice of your inhale and exhale. Close your eyes and physically allow your body to relax from your head all the way to your feet while you consciously shift your focus to inhaling to the count of four and exhaling to the count of four. Repeat this breathing pattern over and over until your entire body is relaxed and your mind is till. Breathe into your mind and allow your inhale and exhale to clear it of outside thoughts, worries and stresses that no longer serve you and can ultimately wait. For the next few minutes you are devoting to yourself.

In this state of mind, you can tap into your mind's eye or intuitive eye. Inhale into that space between your eyes and exhale out. Allow your pineal gland to open and become more aware of your imaginative abilities. See yourself as a hawk perched at the top of a very large, old tree. Become aware of how your talons grasp the branch and how you sit upright, wings resting at your side. You sit calm at the top of this tree. Allow your eyes to shift into seeing binocular vision. This keen eyesight allows you to see further from every angle. You now have the ability to focus with a heightened intensity of perspective.

Sitting perched at the top of this tree, you clearly see everything in fine detail beneath you. Imagine if the landscape below you was a crossroads and each pathway showed a different choice, obstacle, challenge or decision that you are currently facing. Allow yourself to connect with each pathway. If you need to, you can soar down from above and get a closer look. Remember to soar, in this manner you are observing and simply gliding over each pathway as a way of inspecting things from a new perspective.

(Pause)

Really see with a hawk's attentive eye.

Having examined each pathway – choice, decision, obstacle or challenge – which one needs action that you can follow through on? Which one is your top priority? How can you best dive in and grasp this situation, choice, decision or obstacle in the most effective manner? Can you become predator to your own pathway? Are you ready?

Kick off your perch with force and vigor, swoop down and grasp the situation with both talons. Feel how weightless you are as you fly down to take charge of this particular choice, decision or obstacle. Maybe the fact that you felt weighted down by this pathway in the first place and have avoided it until now was all because of how you were looking at it?

Standing at this pathway, your choice grasped in your talons, you are ready to breathe back into your current reality. Feel as your talons become your feet and you stand upright in human form and begin to step one foot at a time on this pathway before you. Make the conscious decision to act on this pathway first, before moving onto the next. Tackle and conquer this pathway before moving on the other pathways on your crossroad, knowing that you can always shift with hawk to gain new vigor and perspective.

Journal Prompts: write down or draw your crossroad. What four things are you currently dealing with or have been avoiding facing that presented themselves in your meditation? Which one stood out the most? Activating hawk's perspective, you were able to dive in and attack the one at the top of your priority list; what does your first step towards accomplishing this look like? What is your follow through?

Hawk medicine is just that, the ability to see further down the pathway and make quick, instinctual decisions. Hawk eyesight is new perspective, being able to disconnect from ego and really see what needs to be done.

GODDESS FRIGG

Welcome the "All Mother", she who sees all, knows all and says very little. Frigg, or Frigga as she is sometimes called, is the wife of the Norse God Odin and mother of Baldur and Hodr. She is Queen of the Aesir and the only goddess permitted to sit beside Odin on the heat seat. A sky goddess, Queen of Heaven, Weaver of the Fates or otherwise known as the Wyrd as a goddess of prophecy. She watches over and protects marriages, relationships and the hearth and home. Her very name is "beloved one". She is regal, serene and calm just like a hawk.

As a weaver of fates, she knows the outcome of all and yet says very little to intervene. She learned this lesson with her son Baldur and his death. Thus she sits like any devoted matron to her family; pondering the choices her children are making and ultimately knowing the consequences.

The Queen Mother archetype is one of poise and love. A love that is strong enough to allow her children to create mishaps and suffer the results of those mishaps and, instead of swooping in to save them and prevent them from heartache or pain, she watches. How many of our mothers would relate to this?

Hawk medicine is very similar. That of the watcher and the one who knows things. Hawks can see and sense prey and predators, yet they hold still and steady until they absolutely have to act. Frigg is the same, she watches and knows, yet doesn't intervene.

Frigg is often called upon to watch over couples as they are joined together in matrimony, handfasted or are about to expand their family with a baby. She is called upon to assist the mother and baby at births, throughout childhood and into adulthood. She is the ethereal mother figure who one can sit and chat with to discuss parental woes and worries. Like a wise one, she sits and listens, only offering wisdom when it is asked for, and if she chooses.

MEDITATION TO CONNECT WITH FRIGG

Begin with your breath, disconnect from outside distractions and allow yourself a quiet space to enter meditation. Take a nice deep inhale to the count of four and exhale to the count of four. Continue this pattern of breath until you are physically relaxed and then allow your eyelids to gently close. Take your focus into your mind and, with each exhale, allow outside thoughts to drift out and away, giving you space to focus and be open to messages. When worries or distracting thoughts surface, simply exhale them out.

Here in this state of relaxation you are ready to go within, deep into your subconscious. You find a large stone structure building before you and, upon entering; you see a beautiful fire is glowing in the hearth at the center. As you approach, you see a very tall, well dressed, poised and serene woman sitting beside the fire spinning wool with a spindle and wheel. She welcomes you to her hearth and invites you to join her beside the fire.

As you sit beside her, she offers you a gentle smile and inquires about your day. There is a calm and gentleness about her and you feel safe discussing the events and happenings that you are currently dealing with. Every so often, she nods and offers a reassuring glance. She listens attentively, yet still continues to spin the wool. You lose all hesitation and feel so safe with her that you settle in next to the fire and offer her stories of you pains, trials and joys.

Sitting here beside her, you relax and ease into a state of wellbeing that you have not felt in quite a while. Your gaze meets the fire and you just watch and relax into a space of being held, comforted and heard. The woman stops her spinning, hands you a horn full of mead, sits beside you and together you both gaze into the flames.

Journal Prompt: when was the last time you were heard? How did it feel to have a listening ear?

Frigg as a mother goddess is very calm and soothing. One can bring all their worries, stresses and challenges to her hearth. While she may not offer suggestions and attempt to help you solve these woes, she will offer you something much more vital; a listening ear.

All too often, when we engage in conversation with others, we become involved in a response and reaction that we fail to actually hear. In this world of social media, oftentimes we do not even put our phones down when someone is talking to us. How can we expect to engage in heart to heart conversations without even making eye contact?

Frigg is a listener, she offers simply a space to unload and be heard. Sometimes that is just what one needs. When releasing and expressing what is going on in our lives, very rarely do we actually seek someone to solve our problems. We are usually wanting to simply unload on them with vocal expression.

The next time you are struggling, go into your meditative space and converse with the All Mother. Open up to her and allow yourself to release through expression. Sometimes a good cry is helpful as well. As Mother Goddess you may feel her hands gently caress your shoulder, lightly touch your arm or she may let you rest your head in her lap as she strokes your hair. You deserve time and space to let go without someone offering you unsolicited or unwelcome advice.

Frigg may also offer you a feather as a reminder that any situation at hand usually is best handled and dealt with by using a new perspective.

FRIGG AS SEIDR

In Old Norse, Seidr is mentioned as a type of magic practiced by the Norse. "Practitioners of seiðr were predominantly women (vǫlva or seiðkona "seiðr-woman"), although there were male practitioners (seiðmaðr "seiðr-man") as well.

These female practitioners were religious leaders of the Viking community and usually required the help of other practitioners to invoke their deities, gods or spirits. The seiðr ritual required not just the powers of a female spiritual medium but of the spiritual participation of other women within the Norse community: it was a communal effort." These female practitioners of Seidr were often referred to as *Volva* which means seeress, prophecy woman or magic woman.

In the *Saga of Erik the Red* these female practitioners led rituals as a way of contacting the spiritual realm through chanting and prayer in times of crisis. These rituals were utilized as a way of looking into the future, cursin or hexing an enemy and for either greater good or daily guidance.

Odin himself, the "All Father", was a practitioner of Seidr which the God Loki taunts and teases him for in the Poetic Edda *Lokasenna*. It is believed that Odin learned this skill and practice from Freya who introduced the Aesir to Seidr. Freya we know to be linked to and oftentimes believed to be Frigg. "Some notable similarities between Frigg and Freyja include the fact that both are attributed to magic. Freyja is related to Seidr (magic, divination) while Frigg is associated with prophecy. Both Frigg and Freyja were joined to similar gods. Freyja was married to the God Ód, and Frigg was married to Odin, both of whom went on long journeys leaving their wives behind. Also, both Frigg and Freyja were thought to have traded their bodies for jewellery, as in the case of Freyja's necklace Brísingamen and Frigg's gold jewellery from the statue of 'Othinus' (Odin)."

However, we also know Frigg to be Goddess of Prophecy and the Fates so her connection with Seidr as "beloved" and the highest ranked queen and the only wife allowed to sit on Odin's thrown, would make it safe to assume that Frigg taught Odin Seidr. Seidr work involved understanding and calling upon the fates, bringing about change and weaving new things into existence.

As "she who weaves" it is only natural to combine both Frigg's Seidr practices with what we know to be modern day witchcraft practices. In fact, some will tell you that, as Volva, a worker of the Seidr is in direct comparison with shamanism and witchcraft and dates back about 2,000–3,000 years ago before the *"Viking Age."* In Nordic societies the Volva's were spiritual leaders and healers. Witch by definition means "one who heals." They were known to go into trance workings and connect with the spirits of other realms in order to answer questions by those in attendance at these rituals, concerning their own fates and futures. The Volva's would also use their Seidr practice for everyday needs, such as healing the sick, controlling the weather or shifting the mood.

When working with or calling upon Frigg to assist with divination, fate workings and seeing into the near or distant future, she offers us hawk medicine as a medium and connection between herself and our mortal world. Volva's were known to amplify the essence and magic of shapeshifting by leaving their body and entering that of an animal.

Oftentimes calling upon a deity can be daunting and at times a turn off due to mainstream religions views on gods as supreme beings with unobtainable qualities or altogether unapproachable. However, you can access gods and goddesses through their animal counterparts. The entire basis of this book is how to work with both as one and the same.

https://en.wikipedia.org/wiki/Sei%C3%B0r

https://thenewpagan.wordpress.com/2014/03/27/frigg-vs-freyja/

https://norse-mythology.net/volva-the-viking-witch-or-seeress/

FRIGG AND HAWK

It is believed that both Frigg and Freya (who are often thought of as one and the same) wore cloaks made of falcon or hawk feathers which gave them the ability of shapeshifting along with the gift of flight. Some say that when Frigg or Freya wore the cloak of feathers they were transformed into hawk and could fly wherever they wished. In the book *The Viking Spirit* by Daniel McCoy he states that, "Freya owns falcon plumes that she and the other Aesir use for shapeshifting into that bird, and Frigg possesses her own set of falcon feathers that are used for the same purpose." I personally choose to embrace the notion that Frigg and Freya are two separate goddesses with similar yet distinct differences and reasons to call upon each as whole unto themselves.

For the ritual below please use a feather that you already have found or have in your possession. It should be noted that owning a hawk feather is illegal in the United States unless you are Native American. You can purchase feathers online via Amazon.com that are decent imitations. You can also obtain an energetic feather or you can paint one. Having an actual feather is not as important as your intent.

Another thing you can use is a shawl that you place over your shoulders when you begin the ritual and enter that space of the in-between.

RITUAL TO CONNECT WITH HAWK THROUGH FRIGG

Altar set up: white cloth, white fur, mistletoe or evergreen sprigs, spindle, feather, statue of Frigg or image.

Herbs: evergreen, mugwort, chamomile (use as loose incense and for smudging).

Gemstones: hawk's eye, place in chalice with blessed water.

Runes: raido and kenaz inscribed on a votive candle.

(The Raido Rune: for lifestyle direction, journey, evolution, new perspective, personal rhythm, dance of life. The Kenaz Rune: illumination, enlightenment, opening up, listening to your intuition, balance of mind, body and soul. Rune used to welcome the light of new perspectives.)

Create the container, cast a circle, call the directions: do this in your own way as this is your solitary ritual.

Call to the Goddess Frigg: "All Mother, she who is calm and comforting. She who stands for social order. She who weaves the strands of fate. Monarch. Queen. She who is patient and kind. Matron of sacred unions. She who protects the lovers. Great healer. She who blesses. Lady that holds the spindle, sacred weavers' sword. Star Mother. Queen of Heaven. She who is prudent and wise. Midwife to Earth. Lady of the Aesir. Goddess Frigg I call to you. Goddess Frigg I honor you."

Chant: "Frigg, Frigg, Frigg."

Ignite the goddess flame: light your candle and spend a few moments adjusting to her energy.

Contemplation: having set intention with hawk to choose a pathway in your crossroad of life, here before your altar discuss with Frigg, as you would discuss with any mother, the choice you have made, the steps you will take and then pause giving her time to connect with you in this space.

Taking flight: from the altar remove the feather and hold it in your hand. Move into a position that is comfortable and simply close your eyes. Frigg offers her hawk feather to those who are ready to shapeshift into hawk and use this medicine to take flight, rise above and see with new eyes. Visualize your flight down the pathway you have chosen and visualize reaching the end, accomplishing the task.

Open the container, the circle and release the directions: in your own solitary way.

Libations of gratitude: offer your sacred herbs to your chalice with the stone and blessed water. Take this water with you to a large tree and leave it as an offering of gratitude to Frigg and hawk.

Journal your experience.

EMBRACING HAWK MEDICINE THROUGH YOGA

Hawk medicine is all about embracing the ability to open your heart chakra and spread your wings to give you a new sense of perspective and insight. One of the best poses for accomplishing this is the ***Supported Fish Pose:***

- There are many ways to set up Supported Fish Pose. The height and position of your blocks will largely depend on the mobility in your thoracic spine. Supported Fish is a great way to gently open up the heart space by allowing your mind to get comfortable with the opposite body pattern most commonly found in everyday life. This pose suggests openness, and this variation is the most extreme in terms of heart opening.
- Set up your two blocks on the highest setting, with the long edge of the block parallel to the short edge of your mat. There should be about six inches between the two blocks. Sit in front of your blocks and slowly recline until you find the first block meet your back. Adjust the block so that it sits at the tip of your shoulder blades. Continue to recline until the back of your skull finds the second block. Lay here for 15 breaths.

Another helpful pose is the ***Bow Asana:***

- Lie on your belly with your hands alongside your torso, palms up (you can lie on a folded blanket to pad the front of your torso and legs). Exhale and bend your knees, bringing your heels as close as you can to your buttocks. Reach back with your hands and take hold of your ankles (but not the tops of the feet). Make sure your knees aren't wider than the width of your hips, and keep your knees hip width for the duration of the pose.

- Inhale and strongly lift your heels away from your buttocks and, at the same time, lift your thighs away from the floor. This will have the effect of pulling your upper torso and head off the floor. Burrow the tailbone down toward the floor, and keep your back muscles soft. As you continue lifting your heels and thighs higher, press your shoulder blades firmly against your back to open your heart. Draw the tops of the shoulders away from your ears. Gaze forward.
- With your belly pressed against the floor, breathing will be difficult. Breathe more into the back of your torso, and be sure not to stop breathing.
- Stay in this pose anywhere from 20 to 30 seconds. Release as you exhale, and lie quietly for a few breaths. You can repeat the pose once or twice more.

https://www.yogajournal.com/poses

CHAPTER THIRTEEN

WOLF

MEDICINE AND MAGICK

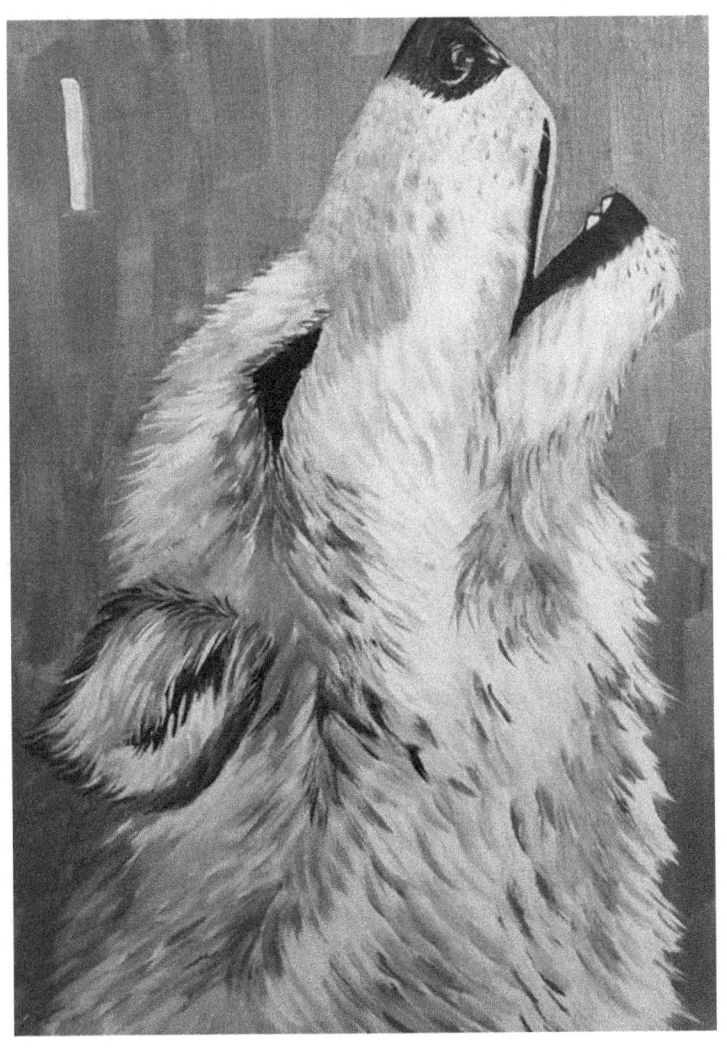

"Those that fear the wolf should not venture into the forest."

RUSSIAN PROVERB

"Where wolf's ears are, wolf's teeth are near."

VOLSUNGA SAGA C.19

Wolf (*canis lupus*) is the largest member of the Canidae family, *canis* meaning dog and carnivore. Canidae includes domestic dogs, wolves, foxes and other extant and extinct species. Wolves are highly intelligent, oftentimes playful, complex and intensely devoted to the social unit of their pack and/or family.

Each wolf pack consists of pups, young adults and/or teens, siblings, aunts, uncles, older wolves that need to be cared for, and a breeding pair, or alpha male and female. Typically each pack has only one breeding pair. The alpha female is "mother of the pack". She is the one who holds everything together. Next in pack line to the alphas are the betas – these are considered second in command to the alphas, then mid-ranking wolves, and finally omegas.

Within this structure of the pack is also a sub-structure of males and females or separate hierarchy for males and females. So there will typically be a beta male and beta female. If something was to happen to the alpha male, the beta male would step up and fulfill that role. What is vital to understand is that each wolf within the pack has their own set of responsibilities and collectively they each fulfill these roles for the safety and well being of the pack as a whole.

"For the strength of the wolf is the pack and the strength of the pack is the wolf."

Together as a pack, each wolf helps to raise, feed and care for the pups. As the pups grow, they look to the other wolves in the pack as examples of how to hunt, what to hunt, when to hunt, how to defend their territory and each member. Wolves care for each others as individuals. They nurture each other and care for each other. Wolves in essence grow together, play together and love collectively which is why their energy is so attractive and calls to so many. When a pack member becomes sick, together they all do their part to comfort, nurture and care for it. When a pack member dies, the entire pack goes through a mourning.

By looking at wolves we can begin to apply their example to us as mirrors – to better serve, protect, build, care for and collectively live together as tribes, clans, extended families, covens and groves.

Wolves are masters at communicating, collaborating and sharing knowledge between generations. The older wolves are more experienced so they teach hunting tips, strategies and techniques to the younger wolves.

Wolves typically live with the pack they were born into for their entire lives. But occasionally young wolves will leave to find mates and formulate their own packs. Others such as the "lone wolves" will forge their own way and disconnect from the pack. A lone wolf is one who is searching and at times, just like humans, it seeks solitude. It is a wolf's nature to belong to something greater than itself, a pack. Wolves form friendships and maintain lifelong bonds. They know that they succeed more when they cooperate and live amongst a pack; they struggle with being alone.

The urge for humans to bring wolf energy into our home comes through the desire to have dogs. Our domestic dogs are genetic descendants of wolves, this is undeniable. What we love about our "pet" dogs is the loyalty and uncompromising love that they offer us as "owners". Dogs are social animals, they take care of their injured loved ones and that includes us, the humans in their life. Dogs are the ultimate companion. A faithful friend. They harness the wolf's territorial defenses and we utilize our own dogs as protectors. Dogs can sniff out and alert us of visitors or intruders who mean us harm. They keep us safe! You can see a lot of the dog in a wolf and a lot of the wolf in your dog.

MEDITATION TO CONNECT WITH WOLF

Begin with your breath. Take a nice deep breath in... and exhale it out... again breath in, really feel your lungs expand and then exhale, pushing all the breath out of your body. One more time, breathe in... hold... and exhale... now go ahead and just close your eyes.

Now breathe in 2... 3... 4... and out 2... 3... 4... repeat three times. Now breathing at your own pace, just breathe fully and easily. Just breathing in and breathing out. Feeling your body relax with each exhale.

Now that you are relaxed, all I want you to do is use your imagination and picture yourself sitting on the ground outside, under a tree in a beautiful forest. Really give yourself permission to see your surroundings. Breathe in the forest. See the trees around you, see the forest floor and feel yourself connect with the ground that you are sitting on.

As you sit here, just take a minute and focus on any areas in your life where you may need to assert more power. Think of a situation that you may be faced with currently or one that you may have apprehension about facing because of fear or a lack of self-confidence. Hold that thought for just a moment.

With that thought on your mind, I want to now focus on the forest and listen carefully. Something is approaching. Know that you are completely safe and that you have chosen to be here. Sitting here in the forest, you begin to see a shape moving towards you, ever so slowly.

Watch the object, as it gets closer you are aware that it is an animal. Not just any animal, but a wolf. Watch as wolf approaches you. What a stunning, majestic, creature wolf is. Watch as this wolf slowly gets closer and closer to you, sniffing you and circling you. Feel the hairs on the back of your neck raising. Wolf is to be respected and appreciated because wolf is a teacher, wolf is the ultimate guide. Now that wolf is here, ask it how to best handle your situation. Maybe wolf will show you how to face your fears, or maybe wolf will agree to stay with you until you have addressed and conquered this situation. Whatever wolf shows you, trust that wolf desires you to be free of anything holding you back in life. Wolf medicine teaches you to trust your instincts, sniff out the situation and know that you will have the confidence, strength and intelligence to face this head on.

When you are ready, I want you to reach out and physically connect with wolf. Either by petting wolf, letting wolf rub up against you, or simply just sitting there with your hand on wolf's back. Feel the power of this animal. Feel the confidence, strength, intelligence and appetite for freedom that this majestic animal has.

Take a nice deep breath in – really breathe in wolf energy. When you are ready, slowly come back to the present knowing that wolf energy will only stay with you if you are in need of it.

Journal your response and meditation experience.

MEDITATION TO SHAPESHIFT WITH WOLF

Allow your eyes to gently close as you bring your awareness to your breath. Take a nice deep inhale and exhale fully. Breathe in and breathe out. Observe how your physical body relaxes each time you exhale, for it is impossible to be tense when you are exhaling. Give yourself permission to relax your forehead, your mouth and your jaw, as you simply continue to breathe in and breathe out. Feel that relaxation move down your neck, your shoulders, your arms, all the way down to your fingertips. Feel as that heavy relaxation moves down to your chest, your stomach and your hips, moving down to your thighs, your calves and your feet. Here you sit, completely physically relaxed.

Bring your focus deeper into your breath. Take a nice deep inhale 2... 3... 4... and out 2... 3... 4... repeat three times. Now breathing at your own pace, breathing fully and easily, your body creates a natural rhythm as you simply breathe in and breathe out.

In your mind's eye feel yourself tucked in comfortably inside a very warm den. The den is covered with fur and it is incredibly warm. You begin to feel as though you are curled up in an almost fetal position. You feel incredibly warm. Breathing into this den where it is very dark you begin to activate your sense of smell. Breathing in deeply you smell dirt, musky and moist. You smell fur. You are smelling yourself... Here in the dark in the den, with your sense of smell activated you begin to move and stretch, only your legs are not human legs, neither are your arms. As you stretch, your eyes have adjusted to the darkness and you see fur, everywhere, all over you. Your feet and hands are now paws with thick padding. You have claws where you once had nails. Give yourself permission to activate and connect with this new form here in the dark. This musky, fur covered animal you know to be wolf.

(Pause)

Let yourself stretch more and more, move around until you are outside of the den. Feel the sun as you stand on all four limbs, connect with the grass beneath your paws and breathe in deeply and breathe out, letting some of your breath escape through your teeth, feeling your lips vibrate. With each breath your senses are heightened and you can smell so intensely you feel a pull to go towards whatever scent has caught your attention. Feel and see as you dig your claws into the grass, finding the dirt beneath. When you are ready; run, run, run! You can go so fast! With all four fur covered legs you are running faster than you have ever run before. You feel completely free, wild and untamed. Running towards a scent drifting on the wind. It doesn't even matter what you are smelling, you are enjoying the run so much! The freedom. The wild. This you!

Bring your run to a stop and feel once more the earth beneath your paws. Bring your nose down to the grass and breathe in the dirt and crisp grass. With your snout to the ground you slowly begin to shed wolf energy. As the fur of wolf falls to the ground around you, your body begins to reveal flesh once more. Your flesh and bones as human returns to your true form.

As you take your next couple breaths you begin to adjust more and more to your form. Connecting with wolf energy invites intelligence, instinct, awareness. Wolf mirrors to us stability. Strength in situations where one could feel threatened or lacking trust in one's self. Wolf energy can be both frightening and calming. All too often people associate wolf energy with dominance and aggression.

Journal your experience: what did it feel like to shapeshift with wolf?

WOLF AS ALPHA

There is a profound misconception with "alpha" ideals. Many times, when wolf comes digging at your psyche and you are called to step into wolf energy, most approach from a state of power, assertiveness and dominion over those they are around. While alpha is the most respected role within the pack; it is not a role of dominance but rather one of service. Just as the alpha female is "mother to all", within a Coven or Grove the High Priestess and High Priest represent the "parents of the community." They are the watchers, those who prepare the way, but the true alpha simply watches, typically from the back of the pack.

When the parents of the wolf pack die, the older offspring assume the parent's role. Within each pack is a social structure and rules of conduct. One of which is respect for the parents. This social structure changes from year to year. Wolves move up in status through a natural selection or "pecking order." The alpha's do not gain their roles through dominance and violence, however.

When there is a need, a predator about the male alpha will step up to defend his own, just as the female alpha will do the same. The males watch over the males and the females watch over the females.

Wolves are for the most part monogamous and a breeding pair will mate for life, with the exception of one of the pair dying; then a new mate will be found. These alpha parents lead by example in a quiet, confident manner. Much the opposite of what most think of when they hear the term "alpha."

In a Coven dynamic, the High Priest and Priestess do the same, they are watchers, protectors and teachers. They are not in an elevated role or position where they are above the Coven or Grove they are in service to the Coven and Grove for the collective good.

Wolf medicine and magic is that of leadership and self accountability. When implementing this attribute into a pack, community, coven or grove it is vital to step into the proper role of wolf as alpha. After all the entire pack, community, coven or grove depends upon the one(s) who birthed it to keep everyone within safe, healthy and thriving.

Wolf medicine is all about the family and pack structure. They are protective, loving and devoted to defending all within their pack, often at the risk of their own lives. The alpha male and female take their role as parents serious.

While a hierarchy does exist within the pack, siblings do bicker and fight with each other on occasion no one within the pack is fighting to achieve or take down the alpha to assume that role. There is already a family order established. It is honored!

Within the pack each member strives to cooperate and is highly skilled at working together with others. If you observe a wolf pack you will not see the ferocious lone "alpha" aggressor. You will see each wolf fulfilling its own role for the sake of the greater good and pack survival.

So why does the term "alpha" encourage some to step into a more dominant, fierce, ego centered way of living and working?

Exercise: in your personal work, how have you activated the misconception of "alpha" and was it purely for self gain? Most likely your answer is yes, you asserted yourself in a form of aggressive dominance to obtain a more elevated position or respect from your peers. However this is NOT wolf medicine or magick. It is quite the opposite. See the aggressor "alpha" in animal form is really in the chimpanzee family not the canine family at all. Let's give credit where credit is due and when you choose to embody the essence or call upon a particular animal, do so in a form of educated respect based on observation and experience.

GODDESS SKADI

Skadi's myth and legend really begins with Odin and his killing of her father the giant "Thjazi" for kidnapping the Goddess Idunna. Skadi, a giantess herself, wanted to avenge her father's death so she stormed into Odin's great hall during a feast and demanded vengeance. Odin being the wise All Father didn't want to battle this great warrior so he wagered a deal with Skadi. At first gold was offered but Skadi was already rich from the pillaging that her father had done. She wanted a husband and a good laugh, as she had not laughed since the murder of her beloved father. So Odin agreed but he had his own twist on the wager.

Odin agreed to let Skadi select a god as her husband on the condition that she select base on only the gods' feet. So the gods stood behind a curtain and only their bare feet showed. Skadi was in love with Odin and Frigg's son Baldur and was certain that he being the God of Light would have the most beautiful feet. However, upon making her selection she had chosen Njord God of the Sea.

Her laugh that she was promised came from Loki the trickster who after many other failed attempts to get Skadi to laugh decided he would tie a rope to the end of a goat and the other end he would attach to his testicles, together he and the goat engaged in a tug of war that ended with much yelping at Loki's expense and when he finally tumbled over Skadi laughed!

Skadi honored her agreement to be married to Njord. Skadi's home was high in the mountain tops of Thrymheim (Thunder Home) a dark, cold peak where the snow never melts. Njord's home was Noatan (the place of ships) a bright, warm beach beside the sea. Both agreed to spend nine nights at each home in an effort to decide where they would ultimately live together as husband and wife.

Njord was miserable in the cold snowy mountain peak with the howling of Skadi's wolves preventing him from sleep and Skadi was miserable with the rocking of waves keeping her awake and the heat from the sun. The two very politely decided to part ways and thus their marriage lasted only eighteen days.

Skadi returned to her cold, snowy mountain top and her wolf pack. It is rumored that she later met the God Ullr and together they were known to ski from village to village in the winters, mingling with the mountain folk. Very little is expressed after this speculation.

One thing is for certain; Skadi the Giantess prefers the company of her wolves and the cold of winter. Skadi is a true warrior. She believes in herself and stands up for what she feels is right. As warrior she does not allow people to talk down to her or disrespect her. She knows her heart and her true worth. So great is her inner strength and outer prowess that even Odin himself made sure to appease her anger before letting her kill every god at his feast which I am certain she would have done in honor of avenging her father's murder.

"A healthy woman is a lot like a wolf: Life-giving, inventive, territorially conscious, loyal, loving."

CLARISSA PINKOLA ESTES

MEDITATION TO CONNECT WITH SKADI

Once again take yourself to your meditative space by connecting with your breath. Inhaling to the count of four and exhaling to the count of four. Repeat this breathing pattern as you consciously move through your physical body and relax each muscle and cell. Beginning with the top of your head, moving to your forehead, your eyelids, allowing each tiny muscle to relax. Let your mouth and jaw go soft, it is natural for your mouth to open as you give yourself permission to relax. Feel this gentle release as each muscle in your neck, your shoulders, your arms, all the way down to your fingertips simply release and let go. Allow your breathing to create its own rhythm with each inhale and exhale. Relax your chest, your stomach, your hips, your thighs, knees, calves, all the way down to your toes as you sit here in a deep state of physical relaxation. Breathe in how good it feels to simply let go of the tensions of the day that you held in your body.

In this state you are ready to go deep within, into your subconscious, your intuitive mind. Some call this your imagination. Allow yourself to connect with this space and give yourself permission to see yourself standing in the middle of the forest. It is winter in the forest so a thick blanket of snow covers the ground upon which you stand. Each exhale you can physically see as it appears you are breathing smoke. While the forest is in winter, you are not cold, you are simply aware of the change in scenery. The trees stand tall and thick around you but their evergreen foliage is sprinkled white from the recent snow storm. It's not quite dark nor is it day, you stand here in the forest at dusk. A time of in-between. The snow has created a sense of calm and the forest is very quiet. Almost unnervingly quiet.

As you adjust to your surroundings you being to feel the chill beginning to caress you. Your breathing becomes more intense and a prickling chill runs up your spine. You know that you must seek some shelter before you freeze. Looking around you see there is a hill just a short distance away from where you stand and there appears to be smoke coming up from the top of the peak. This gives you a glimmer of hope and you strap on your snow shoes and begin to make your way up the hill towards the cause of the smoke.

With each step you get closer and closer, moving up the hill is actually quite easy with your trusty snow shoes. When you reach the peak you see a small cabin with a chimney billowing smoke. You waste no time and approach the snow covered porch. But you immediately come to a stop when you notice the porch is covered with large furry wolves. They have noticed you too but they don't seem bothered by you so while a few perk up their ears, most remain cuddled up in the warmth of their pack.

You cautiously approach the door and just when you are about to knock the door swings open and you find yourself staring at a very inviting fire with a very tall woman crouching over it giving the logs in the flames a stir. You step over a very large and intimidating grey wolf and enter the hearth of Skadi the Goddess of Winter.

As you rapidly rush to the fire seeking warmth, Skadi simply gives you a nod almost as if she is not surprised by a straggler out in the snow seeking the heat of her fire. She invites you to sit but doesn't join you, instead she moves towards the wolf covered porch. Almost as if she prefers the cold over the warm fire. You sit and absorb the heat.

After a while she offers you a cup of mead and asks why you are out in the cold? What are you seeking in the chill of winter? Is it really a warm fire or is there something else?

(Pause)

Bring your attention and focus back to your breath. Keep inhaling and exhaling until you are consciously back in your natural surroundings.

There are numerous reasons to call upon the Goddess Skadi and they should all be of a personal nature. For you are the only one that can determine what it is you are seeking. When we enter Skadi's realm in the wild of winter we are entering the time of darkness, when parts of us hibernate and others awaken. Skadi can be identified with the darker, shadow goddesses. Once winter hits and she freezes the water turning it to snow and ice, the very air around us becomes still. Everything goes quiet.

For some winter can be frightening. They can't escape outside and keep busy. We are oftentimes forced to stay indoors due to inclement weather and things that we normally suppress by being active during the warmer months are now not so easy to suppress. They surface and at times a bit of depression can sink in. We can get very lonely in the winter. Calling upon Skadi, she can help you pin point things that are in need of being addressed or maybe they can freeze for a bit and allow some time to pass before they thaw and you are forced to deal with them.

Maybe it's time to let the sleeping warrior within begin to stir and make plans for what's next. Winter can be a great time to finish projects, do indoor renovations, write, read and do all the other things. The warmth of summer occupies us just enough that we forget about them. Winter is also a great time to plan your garden for spring, set goals and really decide on which way you are going to "warrior" through what some believe to be the most difficult season.

Skadi is linked to the rune "Isa". This rune (I) literally means to push pause, halt, allow to freeze. Ice can freeze and seal in place. Ice holds steady the rushing waters. Have you ever considered doing solitary magick with ice? When a situation or obstacle presents itself and you find yourself unable or just not quite ready to face it, you can write it down on a piece of paper, place it in a jar, fill it with water, close the lid and place it in the back of your freezer to be dealt with at a later time when you step into action and allow the water to thaw. Isa the rune encourages one to be patient, to surrender. Sometimes to surrender and let things sit, halt or freeze can be a surprising act of courage, not to mention wisdom.

Isa can also be an unyielding rune. It can be used as a mirror of resistance. Maybe you are being given time to act finally in the depths of winter but you are resistant. Maybe you are not as fluid as water and you yourself have become frozen with rage, stubbornness or pride? Skadi can be a difficult goddess to embrace; just like wolf she can be frightening and at times cold and unyielding. Skadi's realm of winter offers one silence, isolation. It is okay to feel alone at times, but know that you are part of a much larger pack that is happy to answer your call if you need them. In our solitude we can grow, challenge and become self reliant, which is a vital tool to have. This time of winter solitude can also force you to hold yourself accountable. Just remember, a lone wolf is never lone for long. We too are pack animals and while there are times we MUST retreat into the den to do some pretty serious and at times chilling internal work, our pack is not that far away.

Remember that Skadi is at home in the wild of nature. What does your *wild-ness* look like? We discussed earlier why wolf medicine and magick is so appealing. Skadi and wolf are both very similar. They both possess an unknown and intimidating essence. Is there a part of you that you have kept hidden out of fear of rejection? If you always have a pack that supports you, can you ever really be rejected? Is Skadi's wolf energy howling to you and inviting you to run with the pack or retreat into your den? Is it time for you cuddle up in the warmth of those who keep you safe or go out into the cold of winter and find yourself? Skadi is a warrior goddess and as such she will challenge you in very unexpected ways.

RITUAL TO CONNECT WITH SKADI THROUGH WOLF

Altar set up: white cloth to represent snow, mirror (small handheld one is fine).

Herbs: evergreen boughs to honor the mountain Skadi's home.

Candles: silver and white.

Chalice: filled with snow, ice cubes or ice water.

Gemstones: snowflake obsidian.

Optional items: leather, bow and arrow, wolves, images or statue of Skadi.

Cast your circle, create your container, call the directions: honor your own practice.

Call to Skadi:
"Hail Skadi, Goddess of Winter, she who turns the rain to ice. Snow birther. Hail Skadi, wild one, warrior, she who prefers the solitude of the mountain top. Mother of Wolves. I call to you. Mother of Wolves. I howl to you. Can you hear me?

Hail Skadi, independent, carefree, authentic and free. I call to you with arms open hungry to feel your passion for life and primal wholeness.

Hail Skadi, I welcome your gift of snow, the blanket that tucks in all my cares, worries and reminds me to rest. I honor you Skadi in this your season of winter. I call to you Skadi, teacher, huntress, sister and goddess. Hail and welcome."

Settle in: light your candles, soften your gaze and softly call to her in chant "Skadi, Skadi, Skadi". Do this over and over beginning soft like a whisper and gradually getting louder. Stop when you feel her enter. Allow yourself time to connect with her. Feel her move around you. Feel her wolf pack circle you, sniffing you and cuddling up next to you. In this space you are ready to move your gaze to the mirror.

Looking into the mirror: Skadi and wolf can both be seen in the mirror reflecting back to you vital truths. Can you see the wolf within? Can you feel that wildness clawing from the inside?

- There is no difference between yearning for more and clawing to escape. Is your inner wolf wanting to run wild? Do you have fears, insecurities holding you back? Do you feel like screaming or howling?
- There is no difference between a wolf's howl and speaking one's truth. Sometimes you have to show some teeth, growl a little, maybe nip or bite.
- There is no difference between the wolf's fur and one's clothing, both fulfill the same purpose to provide warmth and protection from the elements.

Shift with wolf: Give yourself permission to feel wolf energy move through you. Closing your eyes, focus first on your breath. With your eyes closed feel your breathing pattern change, you may feel the exhale come out through your mouth almost like you are panting. Allow wolf to move through you. Move around your space like a wolf. Settle in with the wolf pack. Become one of many.

Gratitude: offer the Goddess Skadi gratitude in words, poem or song. To her wolves, offer them the water from your chalice. Offer both Skadi and the wolves a promise to embrace yourself as one and the same with wolf. Promise to use your instincts more, to trust your gut! To sniff a situation out before committing. Offer them your wolf essence as part of their pack.
Release the directions, close the container, open the circle

EMBRACING WOLF THROUGH YOGA

If you do only one yoga pose, this is the pose to do. Downward dog resets the body, mind and spirit. It is energizing, calming, good for your heart and it relieves stress. Not to mention the strengthening and lengthening it physically does for your body. Downward dog is the most well known of all the yoga asanas (poses). This pose is one that you will see wolves and domestic dogs do when they get up from laying down or resting. This is a great pose to do if you have a headache as it is calming to the mind and it increases blood flow to the brain which calms the nervous system.

Step by step moving into downward dog:

- Begin on your hands and knees, keeping your wrists directly under your shoulders and your knees directly under your hips.
- Stretch your elbows and allow your upper back to relax.
- Take a nice inhale and on your next exhale tuck your toes in and lift your knees off the floor. Think of sinking your chest down towards the ground and your pelvis up toward the sky. Your body should make the shape of a triangle. Keep your spine straight and elongated.
- (It is okay if your feet do not rest flat on the ground, move with the pace of your own body and take your time. Remember that there is no perfect yoga body or perfect way to do the pose. The key is in the doing)
- Let your head and neck go soft, relaxing as you focus on your breath.

- With each exhale, move in a little bit more to the pose.
- Hold this pose for about 3–5 breaths release when you are ready.

Transitioning to a seated knee howling wolf pose:

- To move from downward dog to howling wolf simply bring your knees down.
- Place your hands so that they are positioned below your shoulders.
- This pose is called table top.
- From here, move back so that your upper body is now upright. You will be in a kneeling position.
- Allow your hands to slide back on your thighs where they rest at your hips.
- Open up your chest and let your neck and head lean back.
- This is a great position for opening up your heart. It is advised that you give a good howl in this position. Let your throat chakra become activated through the power of sound.

ADDITIONAL TIPS TO DEDICATE OR DEVOTE TO SKADI AND HER WOLVES

As a goddess of the *"wild"*, spending time outdoors is key. Go on a hike! If it is winter maybe take up snowshoeing or skiing. After all, Skadi was known to be married to Ullr the God of Skis. Camping and living off the land for a short or long period of time will definitely reconnect you with Nature, the elements and that wild unknown that makes the Goddess Skadi so appealing. Even though she is a snow goddess and prefers the colder temperatures of the winter season, her season, you can still harness that uninhibitedness anytime you are outside.

Call upon wolf to help you step into the wild. One good way to harness both Skadi and wolf is to go trail running. A simple technique is to take a few moments once you have reached the trail and focus on your breath work. Go into a meditative state and call upon wolf, shift with wolf and you may be surprised at how much faster you can run. If you are not a runner and still wish to feel wolf move through you, why not go outside and get on all fours, move like a wolf would move? If you have a dog, spend some time observing it, how does it move, stretch, walk, run, sleep? Then begin to copy its movement. How does your dog breathe? Can you breathe the same?

Oftentimes the winter can be a very lonely and depressing season for quite a few. We tend to be forced indoors more due to inclement weather. When you are experiencing moments like this go into your bedroom (your den) settle in under the blankets, tuck pillows around you. Close your eyes and visualize a pack of wolves cuddling up around you, maybe even on you. Allow yourself to smell the musky fur, feel the weight of them as they move around the bed with you, feel the heat from their energy as they lay beside you. In this state it will comfort you to know that the Universe is so expansive, even in times where you feel alone, the only thing separating us from the spirit realm is our own ego.

Dedicate yourself to adapting pack mentality. If you lead a community, circle with a group, Coven or Grove, break down everyone's role within your pack. How can each member better serve the collective whole? How can your pack that you circle with reach out, offer service and begin to circle with other packs?

Offering service as a volunteer is a great way to step into pack mentality. Below are wolf rescues across the globe that are always in need of volunteers:

https://wolfsanctuary.co

https://wildspiritwolfsanctuary.org

www.wolfmountainsanctuary.net

Egyptian Animals as Gods

"All things are possible.
Who you are is limited by who you think you
are."

EGYPTIAN BOOK OF THE DEAD

CHAPTER FOURTEEN

COW

MEDICINE AND MAGICK

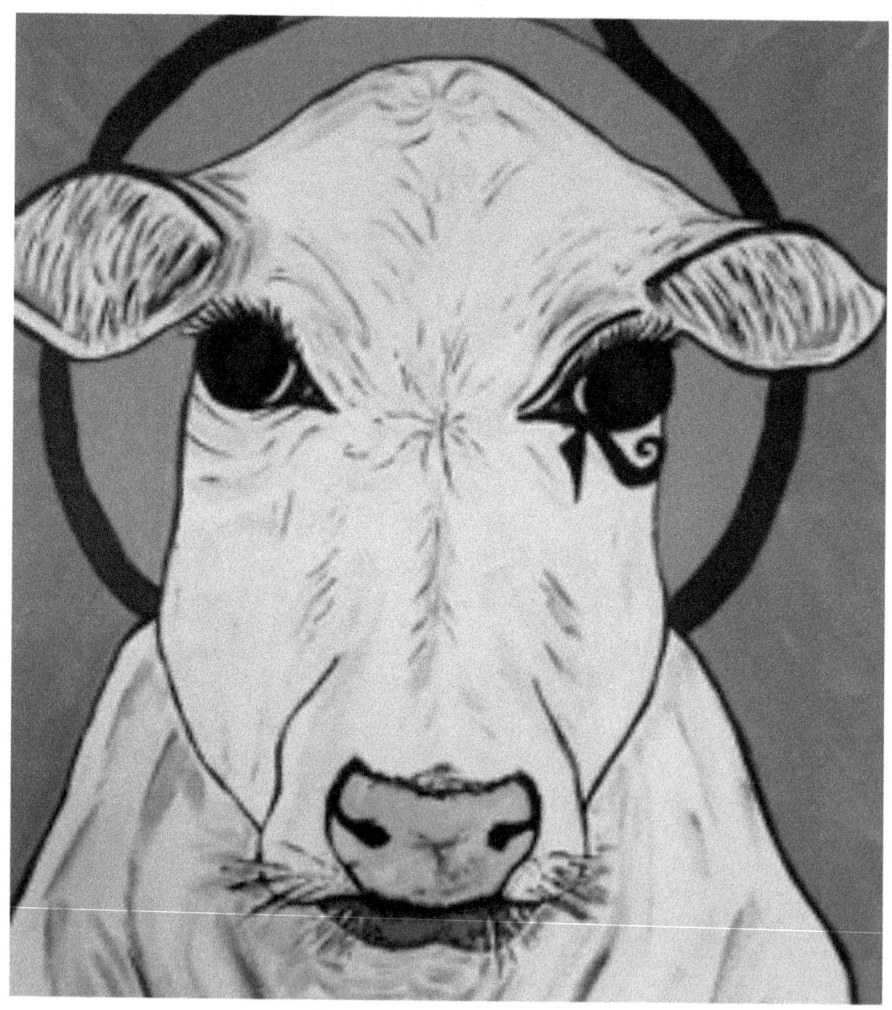

"The cow is the purest type of sub-human life."

MAHATMA GANDHI

"Ancient Egyptian religion was based on polytheism, totemism, animism, anthropomorphism and fetishism."

The dictionary defines these as being:

- Polytheism – the belief in or worship of more than one god.
- Totemism – a belief about the relationship between people and nature.
- Animism – the attribution of a soul to plants, inanimate objects and natural phenomena.
- Anthropomorphism – the attribution of human characteristics or behavior to a god, animal or object.
- Fetishism – worship of an inanimate object for its supposed magical powers or because it is considered to be inhabited by a spirit.

When looking to the Egyptian gods, most were human in physical form with their head being that of an animal. This is a prime example of anthropomorphism. The ancient Egyptians honored animals as sacred, totemic beings. Totemic being defined as – a being that is respected by a group of people, especially for religious reasons and practices.

Let's take for example the cow: large, quadrupedal ungulate mammals with cloven hooves. Most breeds of cows have horns. Cow being the singular terminology and cattle the plural. These large domesticated animals have throughout history been raised as livestock for meat, for milk, for their hides which are used to make leather, they are and have been used to pull carts and plows. Even their dung is used as manure or fuel.

In ancient Egypt cows were honored. To the Hindu's, the cow is considered a sacred animal. An animal that gives life sustaining milk. Cows in India and Egypt are seen as mother figures because of their milk giving properties. While it is debatable as to whether cows are worshipped by the Hindus, they are definitely not slaughtered or used for meat. In fact it is illegal to kill cows in many states in India. Hindus do honor the Vedic scriptures which state that the cow is to be protected and cared for, not eaten. Some Hindus are vegetarians but not vegans as they do use the milk for dairy products which are considered a nutritious and important part of the Ayurvedic diet.

Cows are sacred to other religions such as Jainism, Zoroastrianism, Buddhism, Judaism and Islam. Even the Celts had a Cattle Goddess. The Norse believed and honored the primeval cow Audumbla who gave milk to the ancestor of the Frost Giants. Cows have been cared for since the very first civilizations.

When we look to the Egyptians, their Goddess Hathor was depicted as having the horns of a cow and also would appear as a full bodied cow. In cow form she is known as Hesat and depicted as a pure white cow carrying a tray of food on her head as her udders flow with milk. Hathor was honored as a cow because she was a mother figure who gave sustenance to her people. She is also connected with the primeval divine cow "Mehet-Weret" who is known as a sky goddess and whose name means great flood. Mehet-Weret was thought to bring about the great flood that created the Nile river.

Read more at:

**https://www.shorthistory.org/ancient-civilizations/ancient-egypt/
ancient-egyptian-gods/**

Cows since the beginning of civilization have been givers of life sustaining sustenance. They have been raised for their meat, hides and milk giving properties. Some believe that cows can be directly compared to Mother Earth, for she too sustains us. Cows are for the most part very docile. Cows have been bred to be human kind's prey. We unfortunately live in a time where cows are being bred simply to be consumed. While for our ancestors a cow's properties literally meant life and death to the clans and tribes. Today we are not consuming cows out of need but out of overconsumption. What if we began to see cows as more than just sources of food and sustenance for us? What if we looked at cows in awe and appreciation like our ancestors did? What if we stopped preying on them and started to learn from them? If we allowed animals to once again be our teachers, could our civilization shift away from its current toxic consumeristic state? Could we once again become an agriculturally aware community?

Within a cattle herd there is a hierarchic psychology and behavior that is determined by a natural pecking order or establishment of responsibility. The alpha bull, steer, cow or heifer will be the boss. This is established by assertively staring (maintaining direct eye contact) to the omega or next powerful cow, bull, steer or heifer. Once the stare has been established, the challenge is accepted and a show of physical force follows. This is usually head butting or shoving each other until one wins. The win is determined when one cowers or lowers its head in submission. This continues throughout the herd until every cow understands who the alpha is. What's fascinating is that when one observes a herd or single cow, you can see that they exhibit characteristics that are very similar to a canine's behavior and pack hierarchy.

Cows are incredible at communicating. While most see them as large farm animals that are simply food, cows actually express a wide range of emotions, they are sensitive and they will, much like canines, respond to other animals' (and that includes humans') feelings. For instance, if you are fearful, scared, nervous or frustrated the cows will mirror those feelings all back to you. They are our mirrors!

Cow energy teaches us to be steadfast and stand in one's truth. Cow encourages honor to self as well as a reminder to nurture yourself. Cows are compassionate, tender and loving. They are anchored deep in earth magic. Predominantly they are a symbol of motherhood, fertility, patience and holiness as you the individual would define it.

With cow energy being linked to both earth and motherhood, it is no surprise that she is connected to the Mother Goddess archetype and/or deities associated with earth and motherhood. When calling upon cow for guidance whether as a mirror, totem, teacher, mentor or guide, you will most likely receive motherly advice that you may not always appreciate at the time. But remember you are the one that initiates the call. This symbolism of cow and mother energy can be found in many cultures and pantheons from the Native American tribes, to the Hindus, Celts, Romans, Welsh, Greek and Egyptians.

Cow energy encourages us to stand in our truth. To become self sustaining and to mother one's self for the overall greater good of the herd. This is a gentle encouragement with a bit of softness to it. As an animal that self sustains, remember this can be a mirror to be applied to whatever it is you are dealing with in life right now. When we disconnect from the tunnel vision of a situation, we can better grasp the solutions that are many. Cows have been honored for centuries because every part of the cow is utilized. How can you apply this to your current situation? How can you mother the issues you face that you may seem at a loss to handle? Are you seeing with compassionate eyes? Remember being a child and asking your mother to help you solve a problem? Chances are she offered you many different ways when you most likely saw only one. This is cow energy. Kind, gentle and compassionate.

CONNECTING WITH COW ENERGY

Instead of doing a mediation to connect with cow energetically, seek out a cow. You can use google search, an image from a book, youtube is an excellent source or you can seek out an actual cow. Allow yourself a few moments that are undisturbed and simply sit giving focus to your breath, inhale to the count of four and exhale to the count of four. Put away all sources of distractions only allowing yourself a journal and pen.

With the image, video or actual cow in front of you, allow your breathing pattern to regulate to normal and simply begin to jot down what stands out to you as you gaze at this cow. What physical features stand out to you? Begin to make a list. Be as detailed as you can. Oftentimes when we connect with animals as teachers, mentors, mirrors or guides we focus on the energetic connection or metaphysical properties that we forget that when working with animals the key tool is observation.

As you are making your list, you do so in contemplative mode not critical. You are not jotting down the negative properties or things that you notice. You are diving deeper past the need to judge and tear down. This need to tear apart or physically point out flaws is something that we as humans reserve for other humans. Isn't it interesting that with animals such as cows we don't really have this tendency? However, with our fellow herd or pack of humans this kind of behavior is second nature.

This is why working with animals is so vital! The more we begin to embrace, see and allow animals to have their unique and distinctive differences, the more we can begin to implement this behavior when dealing with our own kind; or at least that is the hope.

With your list of physical attributes written down, let's begin to write down how cow emotionally makes you feel. Do you feel calm or compassionate? Do you feel appreciation? How about adding to the list all the things that you have in your possession that came from a cow? What foods are in your fridge or pantry that come from cows? Be as detailed as possible.

As you spend time in observation mode, can you possibly see why the ancient clans revered and honored these large beasts? How about making a list of all the ways they may have used them in their primitive communities? When you really sit and formulate a list of all the ways a community survived because of the sustaining attributes of an animal, it puts things into a new perspective. A perspective of appreciation.

The ancient clans knew and understood that the health of their livestock meant their very survival. Here in our modern world of privileges we very rarely sit and give thought to where our cheese, milk, butter, leather and clothing comes from. By stepping into a more conscious way of living and by being more aware and making lists such as this one, you can shift your life into a more present, involved and educate the areas of your life that have become mundane or something to take for granted.

With deep observation comes deep appreciation. When we remember that this planet is shared by all and that animals are not to be owned as property, we can shift into a greater awareness of how much we are all interconnected. As Ghandi said, "Cow protection to me is infinitely more than mere protection of the cow. Cow protection means protection of the weak, the helpless, the dumb and the deaf. Cow protection to me is one of the most wonderful phenomena in the human evolution. Mother cow is in many ways better than the mother who gave us birth."

GODDESS HATHOR

Egyptian primeval Goddess from whom all life began. Mother of the Sun God Ra. Patron Goddess of Joy, Celebration, Love, Compassion and Fertility. Goddess of Sky and Earth. Mistress of Life, Lady of Necropolis and she who opened the gates of the underworld. Tree Goddess. The one who shines as brightly as gold. Mistress of the Desert. Lady of Heaven. Mother to the Gods. Goddess of the West. She who welcomes the setting sun into her outstretched arms. Goddess of re-birth. Golden Goddess. Mother of Mothers. Goddess of Women. Hand of God. Lady of the Vulva.

Hathor was depicted as a woman with a head of a cow, ears of a cow, or simply as a cow. She is one of the most famous and well known of the Egyptian gods. As we have seen, she is known as the "Great one of many names." Linked with the Goddess Nut, Hathor to some is believed to be a personification of the Milky Way. This universal reminder that milk flowed from the udders of a heavenly cow. More festivals were dedicated to her and more children were named after her than any other deity of Egypt. Hathor was so well loved that her worship extended to Nubia, West Asia, Ethiopia, Somali, Libya and Byblos.

Hathor was loved, adored and worshipped by not only the wealthy but commoners as well. Even the Pharaohs of the New Kingdom (1150c. – 1069 BC) looked to her as Supreme Mother. The earliest depiction of Hathor dates back to the pre-dynastic era. Many statues of Hathor date back to the reign of Amenhotep II (1427c. – 1400 BC). The first shrine of Hathor existed in the pre-dynastic period. During the reign of Khufu (2589c.- 2566 BC) it was rebuilt. There are many temples dedicated to Hathor all over Egypt. The most well-known is located in Dendra. Even in the Temple of Philae, which is built in honor of the Goddess Isis, sits a shrine in honor of Hathor. It was in this temple that Hathor was honored as Goddess of Music and Dance.

Hathor's symbol or instrument is the sistrum. This instrument is similar to a tambourine and commonly known as a rattle. This instrument was believed to be magic. There are stories of it being used to stop the flooding of the night, to frighten Seth away for he was the god who brought chaos, storms and violence. When Hathor would shake her sistrum, it was to welcome the gods and drive away evil. Isis as mother and creator was often depicted holding a sistrum. The sistrum was also used as a way of worshipping musically several Egyptian gods including Amon. Sistrums were adopted by the Greeks after Rome's conquest of Egypt in 30 BC, more as a symbol used at festivals and funerals.

Hathor as Mother Goddess was also known as watcher of women, protectress of women from infant, youth to adulthood. She was said to help as new babes entered this realm and later to assist them in crossing over into the underworld. Many view her as a triple goddess since she is well known for honoring the three main phases of womanhood. Women would call to Hathor when they were seeking a husband, wanting to conceive a child and during birth. She was also a protector of lovers and known as a goddess of sensuality and fertility.

Hathor had many priestesses which was fairly uncommon as this put women as equals to the male priests. Her priestesses were typically depicted in red dresses with red scarves and beaded menat necklaces. These priestesses were often thought of as prophets, oracles and midwives. Many were dancers, actors, singers and musicians who utilized these talents in rituals that were works of art. Belly dancing was a gift of celebration in honor of Hathor and the ability of the woman's body to grow large with life and give birth.

There are many reasons to call upon any specific god or goddess. When it comes to Hathor you can focus on calling upon her to assist you in achieving motherhood, when you are in need of mothering guidance, or when you have neglected yourself and need to nurture and do some serious *self mothering*. As a goddess who is supreme in her sexuality and confident in her abilities to rule and have both priests and priestesses in a time where women were not typically in that elevated position, calling upon Hathor as a deity of equality would be beneficial. Or maybe you need to activate your sexual prowess through dance? A very simple way to call upon her is through dance, music and the arts. Sing her name!

RITUAL ACTIVATION TO CONNECT WITH HATHOR

If you have felt the motherly call of Hathor and wish to connect with her, devoting time, energy and physical space are all ways to activate and move towards answering this call. Spend some time setting and creating your intention to call upon the "Mistress of Life."

Altar: red or white cloth. Red for passion, sexuality and dance. White for purity, calm and new beginnings.

Gemstones: turquoise, malachite, gold, copper.

Incense: myrrh or frankincense.

Candles: red, white, gold.

Herbs: myrtle, sycamore, grape leaves, mandrake, coriander, rose petals.

Libations: red wine, beer, bread.

Music: any!

Once you have created your altar, cast your circle, create your container and make sure that you remove any distractions. Remember that you have consciously set the intent to work with Hathor so follow through by setting some time aside, free from outside distractions. It's always a good idea to let those who you live with know that you will need to be left alone for the next hour or so. This act of setting boundaries is vital in confirming your intent to call upon an ancient deity. For some, working with the Egyptian gods can be a bit unnerving as they are beyond ancient. However, as a ritual priestess, it is my belief that anytime you call upon any of the gods or goddesses you should do so from a place of humble respect. After all, you are calling upon them for something, whether it is guidance, insight or as a mirror. Do so with a tad bit of tact and thoughtfulness. Turn off the lights and ignite your candles!

Turn on your selected music and now that you have created your space, move your body. Hathor is a goddess of dance, music and sexual freedom. While it is not vital to dance it is often very liberating and remember why you are calling upon her in the first place. How do you wish to embody the essence of this ancient mistress of life? Dancing is a form of trance, meditation and worship. When you are in a space that is isolated from disruption you can really let loose. For this ritual, dance is the form of connection. You can say her name over and over again while you move your body. The more you lose yourself in dance the more intense the connection. Allow yourself to disconnect from ego and enter the present moment, there is no judgment here in the dark with only candles lit. Just Dance!

When your dance is complete and you feel *her* presence, sit with her. Gaze into your flickering candles and talk to Hathor as you would your mother. Or maybe now is the time to embrace her as the mother you have always wanted and thought you needed? Either way, talk to her. Pour out your emotional woes to her, your joyous celebrations, your dreams, wants and desires. Lay them at her feet. Harness the freedom of a calf and gift yourself time to be completely present. Allow yourself some time to absorb any response, energy or guidance she may offer. Then offer libations in her honor, drink and eat of them yourself. Feast and/or drink with Hathor.

Take as much time as you need, this is your connection. Then, when you are done, bid her farewell in your own way and open your container, open the circle and come back into your conscious reality. Take some time to journal your experience and any insight you may have gained or received.

EMBRACING COW AND HATHOR THROUGH YOGA

Cow pose or Bitilasana is a great pose or asana for warming up the spine which is the lifeline to longevity. This pose is most often done in conjunction with the cat pose which is ironic or coincidental since Hathor is also seen in many myths and legends as the Goddess Sehkmet who is a Lion Goddess. The two deities are typically always referenced together.

Hathor and Sekhmet, are they one in the same? It is said that after Sekhmet consumed most of humanity in a rage of defense in honor of Ra she was tricked into a drunken stupor and when she awakened three days later she was in such a state of humility that she became Hathor. You could say that Sekhmet is Hathor's shadow self or that both represent the turning of the wheel and the change of the seasons.

Step by step:

- begin on your hands and knees.
- on your inhale allow your shoulder blades to come together, let your pelvis tilt up and your back go swayback, tilt your head up and back.

- on your exhale round out your back, tuck your head and chin towards your chest.

In your yoga practice these two poses when combined focus you into being fully present and calm. They gently stretch your abdomen and hips. By shifting from one to the next on each breath inhale for cow and exhale for cat you shift your mind into a state of calm, which relieves stress. Just like cow energy is very calming emotionally, the cow pose in yoga is very calming, soothing and healing physically.

This movement of cat/cow through yoga can be used in place of dance in the previously mentioned ritual. It is recommended that these two poses be used together as a warm up to any yoga practice. If you want to live a long healthy life any yogi will tell you that it all starts with the flexibility of your spine.

MEDITATION CONNECTION WITH HATHOR AS COW

Sitting in a nice comfortable position, just focus on your breath. We begin with a unified inhale and exhale fully. Breathe in and breathe out. Giving ourselves permission to simply focus on our breath, keeping us in the present moment. Every time an outside thought enters your mind simply breathe it away on your next exhale. Breath in 2...3...4... and out 2...3...4... (repeat 3 times).

In this state of relaxation you are calm, relaxed and at peace. Feel yourself returning to Egypt. Feel the desert sands beneath your feet, feeling the warmth and heat as it moves through the soles of your feet up your legs, your hips, your torso, your chest, your arms, your neck, feeling the heat move all the way up through your face and out the top of your head. Literally soaking up the heat of the desert. Feel the warmth of the sun on your face and breathe in this heat.

(Pause)

Before you stands Dendera the Temple of Hathor, "the Great One of Many Names." You see the six large stone pillars with her image engraved upon them. Standing in front of this massive stone temple, you begin to feel a sense of deep love. In ancient time's people would travel great lengths to reach this temple for its healing powers. You too are in need of healing. Everyone is.

You walk along the stone pathway and enter the main room of the temple. You hear music and song birds singing. You ascend the spiral staircase that leads up onto the roof where there is a chapel filled with columns of stone with Hathor's image carved into them. The chapel is lit with candles and there is an altar in the middle with offerings that people over the years have left in honor of this great goddess of love, healing, fertility and joy. You reach into your pocket and pull out your offering and gently place it on the altar. The chapel room is very quiet and the energy is very calm and sacred. There is a power here that is beyond description but feels your soul with a great knowing and great love.

(Pause)

As you leave the chapel and descend down the spiral stairs, exiting the temple you return outside and even though the sun has begun to set it is still quite warm. You begin to walk down the stone pathway leaving the temple grounds when you see before you a very large white cow. Even in animal form, you recognize the Goddess Hathor immediately. You can feel your grounding, safe and loving energy. Gazing as this large cow, you stand in awe. For though it is modern times and you are only a tourist here in Egypt, you remember when you lived here centuries before and you remember her in her true form. You have not forgotten the ancient goddess. Nor has she forgotten you.

For here she stands in the form of a cow. Docile, tender and merciful. You feel safe as you approach her. You reach your hand out to her and softly stroke her forehead, behind her ears and her upper back. Her eyes large and intense gaze into your very core. Almost as if she is energetically holding you. Simply by touching her she heals you. Taking away all your pains, worries and stresses. She fills you up with peace.

(Pause)

She slowly walks past you as your hand grazes down her back. You feel relaxed, whole and inspired. For to touch the Goddess Hathor is to awaken and spark your creative passions. Take a deep breath here and focus on something that you have always wanted to create. It could be a craft that you have always wanted to conquer, a poem or story you have always wanted to put into words, a painting you haven't finished, a song that is bursting forth and needs to be written...Whatever it is, focus on it having a new breath of life.

(Pause)

When you are ready, take a nice deep breath in and exhale it out. Bring your focus back to your breath. Feel Egypt slipping away into the distance with each exhale, knowing you simply need to close your eyes to visit again. Feel each breath anchor and ground you back to the present moment. Feeling your fingers and toes, begin to move as you slowly come back to the room, filled with a sense of peace, motivation and creative spark.

Journal your meditation.

www.nationalgeographic.com/news/2018/01/egypt-tomb-woman-priestess-hetpet-

https://ancientegyptonline.co.uk/hathor/

CHAPTER FIFTEEN

LION

MEDICINE AND MAGICK

"A lion sleeps in the heart of every brave man."

TURKISH PROVERB

All hail the king of the jungle, the ruler of all beasts. No other animal captures strength, power and courage quite like the lion does. These majestic animals have been symbols of royalty dating back about 3,000 years BC. Several monuments, carvings and artifacts confirm that our ancient ancestors had a profound respect for these great beasts.

There are numerous temples with large lion statues and artifacts serving as protectors and watchers of the gateways or entrances. Such as the "Lion Gate" in the south west of Hattusha, the capital of the kingdom of Hittites. At the Ishtar Gate in the near east there can be found a large gate decorated with colored tiles in the form of a lion. There is also the famous lion gate at Mycenae in Greece, to name but a few.

Most of us are familiar with the iconic image of the Sphinx which is a large statue with a human head and lion's body. The Sphinx represents a guardian and keeper of sacred temples. The oldest Sphinx dates back to 9,500 BC in Gobekli Tepe in Turkey. The Sphinx can be found in medieval churches and tombs from all over Greece, Mesopotamia, Egypt and the Mediterranean. There are different meanings and slight differences in design but overall the consensus is the same; these mystical creatures of lion and man held power for the ancients.

The very first cave painting of a lion was found in France in the Chauvet Cave, this Paleolithic cave art dating between 32,000 and 15,000 years ago. The oldest animal shaped sculpture ever found was a half human half lion carving made from the tusk of a mammoth during the upper Paleolithic period.

The lion is the symbol of Scotland and there are three lions for England. Some scholars believe that we have Richard I "the Lionheart" to thank. The lion was derived from the coat of arms of the Duchy of Aquitaine, it was Eleanor of Aquitaine who married Henry II and was Richard's mother. The Lion was thought to best personify the British attributes of courage, strength, dignity and pride.

If the lion is king of the jungle, couldn't the lion also represent the ability to be king of one's self? In order to reign as a king over any country, a desired attribute would be to set aside one's personal gain, worries and emotional struggles for the greater good of the people. We know Richard the Lionheart to be one of chivalry and rebellion against his father. Can we actually compare his accomplishments to the attributes of a lion?

In India the Emperor Ashoka has two stone lion pillars that represent a gentle fearlessness. African cultured songs are sung in praise of those with *"lion-like"* courage. In Trafalgar Square in London there are four enormous bronze lions that stand at the foot of Nelson's Column. The artist Saint Jerome often used lions as companion animals in his paintings. A bronze winged lion is the symbol of Venice.

The Hindus honor a half lion half man god Narasimha, his consort is Kali the destroyer. In religion the lion merged with the human gods such as Vishnu and even Jesus. So it actually makes sense why lions are revered and honored as kings.

CONNECTING WITH LION ENERGY

These great beasts once roamed all over Africa, Asia and Europe but now are only found in parts of Africa and India. Lions are now considered "vulnerable" which is one step away from being endangered, this is according to the IUCN Red List. The West African lion is listed as critically endangered. The largest threat to the African lion population is the import of lion parts to the US. This makes the United States the largest threat to the population of the African lion. Large "safari hunting parties" and trophy kills have and continue to threaten the African lion population. We all remember the killing of "Cecil" the lion who was shot by an American dentist who was participating in a "pay-to-shoot" safari. With our global population of humans struggling for survival amongst the 2020 pandemic of the Corona virus (which is believed to have stemmed from the consumption of a wild animal) we as humans have a vital obligation to end these disgusting and detrimental, not to mention barbaric practices of slaughtering wild animals as trophies and exotic cuisine.

The African lion from head to tail measures nine to ten feet. They typically weigh anywhere between 300 to 500 pounds. Asiatic (Asian or Indian) lions are a bit smaller, measuring from head to tail between six to nine feet and weighing between 200 to 400 pounds. The males are generally larger with a mass of thick hair around their heads. Their mane protects their necks during territorial fights and mating rights. The African lion has a much larger mane compared to the Asiatic lion.

We generally think that it is the large male with the exotic mane that leads the lion pack or "pride" as they are called, but in actuality it is the females of the pride. They are the hunters, they guard and protect their territory and the males come and go. The males do however travel together so that they can protect each other. It is the females of the pride that determine which males are allowed to stay. So a typical lion pride consists of primarily related females (aunts, daughters, sisters, mothers), the male is from another pride altogether. The females select which males can stay for mating based upon their looks, how strong they are and ultimately who has the best mane. They form the stable common core of the entire pride.

So why is it we automatically are drawn to the large male as the "King of all Beasts?" Shouldn't we look to who keeps the pride going? That being the Lion Queen and her sisters and daughters. Or is that too matriarchal for our modern society? Has it become the norm to associate males with the defenders and rulers?

Going back to lions and royalty, can one embody the essence or attributes of lions in their everyday life? How can we be kings and queens of our own castles? Well, looking to the female lions, they are very protective of their young, each other and their territory. How are you in need of more protection? Or what can you do to protect yourself, your pride and your home? This desire to protect can also be related to bravery and courageousness. Lions are the only big cats to embrace pack life by living in large groups. So how can you apply this mindset to your current living situation and conditions? How can you as ruler of your own day to day serve and protect not just yourself but your own "pride"?

When embracing lion as mirror, it is again very important to participate in some form of observation. There are numerous videos online, movies and articles you can read that discuss the attributes and way of lion life. What comparisons can you make? What similarities and differences stand out? How can you utilize both in gaining not only respect but deep appreciation for these magnificent creatures that most often are now only seen as trophies? Do you like that mirror? Do you want to be seen simply as a trophy? I seriously doubt it!

Before we dive into a meditation connection with lion, let's physically activate the strength of lion through movement and yoga. The lion pose in yoga, or Simhasana as it is called, is designed to strengthen the lungs and throat. Think of your throat chakra and your ability to speak your words truthfully. This pose also activates your immune system response, calms stress and tension. This pose has been said to "nurture the freedom of your soul." It is also known as the "destroyer of diseases." Physically it tones the neck, helps with digestive issues and respiratory issues.

Step by step into lion pose:

- kneel on the ground; your knees should be about hip width or more apart.
- you can cross your ankles if you wish or leave them uncrossed.

- sit back.
- place your palms on your knees applying slight pressure.
- keep your eyes open and gaze forward.
- exhale through your mouth with your tongue sticking down and out making a "ha" sound, this breath should come from your diaphragm.
- do this inhale and exhale for a few minutes, really allowing yourself to "roar" with each exhale.

If you suffer from knee issues, you can do this pose sitting in a cross legged position or half lotus pose. You can also do this position standing. Do this breath work anytime you are feeling congested, angry or stressed. Over time you will begin to feel the anger and stress decompress as you step into your physical and mental strength. Lion pose should be a part of your everyday self care practices. It is also a very good pose for children who struggle with stutters, insecurities and inability to express vocally what they are in need of.

Moving into a meditative activation with lion energy, it is highly recommended that you create a den or physical space where you will undisturbed. Think of how cats behave when they are in need of rest or isolation and embody that. You can arrange pillows or your favorite blanket in a way that would be similar to a large cat getting ready to take a nap. Crawling and moving like a lion will also help your body prepare to activate catlike energy into your physical and mental capacities.

MEDITATION TO CONNECT WITH LION

Beginning with your breath, allow your eyelids to gently close and focus on each inhale and exhale begin at least four counts. Take some time to mentally move through each part of your body, releasing any tension and allowing yourself to enter a complete state of relaxation.

In this state you can easily tap into your mind's eye, that place where your imagination reigns wild and free. Imagine yourself as a very large cat, one of the largest cats – a lion. Breathe your human form into the strong muscular, lean form of a lion. It doesn't matter if you are of masculine or feminine form, it only matters that you subconsciously embody lion.

With your eyes closed, begin to move your physical body the way a lion would move. Stretch slow and precise. While you stretch you become aware of the desert grasses that you are lying upon and you stretch into them, feeling them brush against your fur. As you dig your massive claws into the ground you feel the sand move with you. Allow yourself to roll onto your back. Completely relaxed, you feel the heat of the sun against your fur, it is both healing and helps you relax even more.

In this state as lion you are filled with confidence and you know you are strong. Anything and everything is possible. You may feel other lions approach and rub up against you, lying beside you, pawing at you. This is your pride. Allow yourself to connect with the other lions, who is in your pride that you feel the most comfortable around? These are your loyal and most trusted companions. Feel their energy connect with yours as you and your pride begin to stretch up from the ground and break out into a run. See them running beside you. Feel them running beside you. Always supported. Never alone. This is freedom! When you are able to be your complete uninhibited self with others that are completely themselves, you are all free!

Slow your run and come to a standing stop on all fours position. Breathe back into your human surroundings, bidding the desert goodbye and your fellow lion pride farewell. Knowing you will see them in human form and recognize their energy, loyalty and support. Take a nice deep inhale and lengthen your spine, reaching from lion form into human form. Focusing on your breath and allowing each inhale and exhale to move you back into your true form in this existence, taking with you the confidence of lion. You open your eyes and gently tap into your arms, legs, tapping your physical body back to a healthy, awakened and human form.

Journal your meditation connection with lion.

HAIL SEKHMET – THE LIONESS GODDESS OF EGYPT

As we have learned in the pride of lions, it is the females that hold the center, rule and keep the pride safe and thriving. So it is no surprise that the Queen of the Desert Sun of Egypt is a Lioness.

Sekhmet, she of a thousand names! Powerful one, Sun Goddess, The Scarlet Lady, Goddess of War, Goddess of Destruction, Goddess of Plagues and Healing, Goddess of the West, Mistress and Lady of the Tomb, The Gracious One, The Destroyer of Rebellion, The Mighty One of Enchantments, The Eye of the Sun God Ra, The Goddess of the Hot Noontime Sun. Sekhmet is one of the most powerful Goddesses of Egypt.

So feared and honored that she is estimated to have over 700 statues of her in the Temple of Amenhotep III. It is believed that in order to calm her wrath, the people of Egypt performed a different ritual in the presence of a different statue every day of the year.

She is the one Egyptian deity who has the most statues built in her honor. In the magical tradition there were as many as 4,000 names or epithets of her. These were words of power used in the practice of initiation and meditation on the goddess.

She is depicted as a tall woman, dressed in a long red gown with the head of a lioness. She is seen as a goddess of great importance and magnitude. Her power, much like the Celtic queen The Morrigan, is both derived from light and dark. She is Goddess of Kundalini energy symbolized by the royal cobra which she bears on her head together with the solar disk. She was a conduit of the psychic energy of "Shakti", this boundless cosmic energy that gifted her with all her power. Shakti by definition is the female principle of divine energy, especially when personified as the supreme deity. Shakti is the powerful creative energy inside each of us.

Some scholars say she was born when Ra, who was angry with humankind for their disrespect, ripped out his eye and threw it at the people of Memphis. His discarded eye turned into Sekhmet who, in the form of a great lioness, began to avenge Ra by killing and butchering the disrespectful humans. She drank their blood and enjoyed her slaughter immensely. Ra seeing this act of vengeance knew that she would consume the entire human race. He tried to calm her, but she refused to be sedated. So he tricked her into drinking the River Nile which he turned red with beer and pomegranate juice. Sekhmet drank excessively and fell into a drunken sleep. She slept for three days. Some believe that after her drunken stupor she awoke and was so humbled that she became the docile Mother Goddess Hathor.

Humankind celebrated being saved from the wrath of Sekhmet and in commemoration each year they drank beer stained red with pomegranate juice.

Sekhmet was known throughout Egypt as the fierce huntress. Her breath was said to have created the desert. She was the great protector of the Pharaoh's. The Avenger of Wrongs. Goddess for Women.

Most people call to Sekhmet when they are in need of reminding of their own strengths. Sekhmet is a mirror of intimidating power, strength and confidence. She is the burning, scorching, destructive heat of the sun, a force to be both respected and at times feared.

As a lioness, she offers confidence to face the challenges ahead. The loyalty of the pride. She offers wisdom, strength, mirror of leadership and source of motivation. She roars loudly to be bold, be wise and be fierce in the things that are your truths.

The color red – excerpt from Candace Kant's book "Heart of the Sun

– An Anthology in Exaltation of Sekhmet" she states, "Often referred to as The Lady of Red linen, Sekhmet wears a close fitting dress that reaches to her ankles. The color red links the ideas of life and regeneration with fire, blood and the ochre-colored funerary henna. The word for red (desher) formed the word desert (deshret) meaning the red land. In contrast to the black land, which was fertile and habitable, the red land was dangerous and unpredictable. "Wrath" (desheru) associated with Sekhmet through the myth of the destruction of humanity, had its roots in the word "red". Thus the color red was associated with anger and destruction, signifying the fierce nature of the radiant sun, and as such the color was used for the serpent amulets representing the Eye of Re, the fiery protective and potentially destructive aspect of the sun deities. The color red also signified the beginning of life. When the yearly inundation of the Nile began, the waters looked greenish before they turned an opaque, dark ruddy color from the type of red algae pushed out of the central African tributaries and downriver by the melting snow and flood waters."

The color red is energizing. It excites emotions and motivates us to take action. It signifies leadership, ambition, determination, strong will, sexuality, passion, lust, assertiveness, violent brutal revenge, anger and the power to awaken our physical life force.

RITUAL TO CONNECT WITH SEKHMET

Altar set up: red cloth, red candle.

Ritual attire: long red robe or dress.

Incense: myrrh, frankincense, cinnamon, sandalwood, orris.

Gemstones: carnelian, citrine, amber, topaz, tiger's eye, ruby, garnet, red agate.

Libations: beer, pomegranate juice.

Sekhmet: ankh, statue, lion, or image.

Create your altar in your own way. Set aside some time to devote to ritual as you would normally do in your solitary practice. Turn off any distractions and let those that you live with know ahead of time that you will be doing ritual, so that you will be undisturbed. Take some time before you begin your ritual to focus on your intent. Why are you wanting to call upon Sekhmet? Create your container; cast your circle in your own way.

Once your container is set and circle cast, light your red candle. Ignite your incense of frankincense and myrrh onto a charcoal disk in a fire proof container or burner. When you are ready to call upon the Goddess Sehkmet, there are many invocations you can do. The best are of course your own words. Remember there are many, many ways, no one way or right way. This is your ritual and your connection to it should be authentic. I typically call to Sekhmet through her chant "Sa Sekhem Sahu". Sa-the breath of life/life force, Sekhem-the source, Sahu-the spirit."

INVOCATION TO THE GODDESS (IF YOU WISH TO USE IT)

Sekhmet, Great One of Magic, Mother of the Gods, Lady of the Place of the Beginning of Time, Roamer of Deserts, Opener of Ways, Giver of Ecstasies, Satisfier of Desires, Ruler of Lions, Sublime One, Destroyer of Fire, Complete One, Mistress of the Lady of the Tomb, The Source, The Aware, Lady of Jubilation, mightier than the gods, Protectress of the Divine order, Goddess of Love, Devouring One, one before who evil trembles. Hail and welcome beloved Sekhmet.

Allow yourself to connect to her energy. Sit at her feet and slowly bring your focus to your breath. Taking a slow deep inhale and exhaling fully. Breathing in focus and allowing your body to relax with each exhale. Breathe in 2... 3... 4... and out 2...3...4... (repeat four to six times).

Breathing at your own pace, breathe fully and easily. See yourself returning to the desert. This time you are in human form. Feel the sand beneath your feet. Feel the heat of the sun on your face. Feel your legs as they begin to trudge through the deep sand moving forward, seeking the temple of the Great Lioness Sekhmet, Goddess of Destruction, She most powerful.

Feel yourself ascending the sandstone steps in front of you and move towards the large ornate entrance of her shrine. As you walk through the doors the hall is lit by numerous candles and there is a large fire pit with golden flames blazing in front of a very large statue of the goddess. You can feel the energy radiating in the room as if this statue is embodied with the very essence of Sekhmet herself.

You slowly approach, feeling the heat of the fire as you move closer and closer towards the statue. Her eyes watching you the entire time. You feel as if the statue is coming alive. You kneel at the feet of the statue and softly begin to chant "Sa Sekhem Sahu" over and over again.

When you feel overwhelmed by energy you look up at the statue and see that *She* has awakened. Take a deep breath and allow yourself to connect with Sekhmet the Mighty Goddess. Take note of how the statue moves and approaches you. What have you come here for? Now is the time to ask her for strength. Now is the time to express to her what it is you are in need of overcoming? Why have you come to her Temple? Why have you awoken her?

Take some time to really connect and converse with the goddess. Once you feel complete, offer her a libation of ale at her feet. If you feel inclined, express in your own words a verse, poem or song of gratitude.

See yourself standing up and slowly walking away. Leaving the safety of the temple and venturing once more into the sands of the desert. Feel the sand beneath her feet as you take in a nice anchoring breath and exhale fully.

Give yourself permission to come back to the present. Feeling the confidence and strength gifted to you by the Goddess Sekhmet. Take another deep inhale and exhale. Allow each breath to bring you back to the room, feeling anchored, balanced and in control of your life.

Allow some time to pause and then journal your ritual experience.

LIBATION TO SEKHMET BY QAISET

"My Lady Sekhmet, Great one, Eye of Ra.
One of power and destruction.
Great lioness of the sun, and the sands and the winds,
Divine Lady of Ma-at, Mistress of Life.
Long have you bestowed upon me
your glory and magnificence. Your lessons and
your guidance, your shining divine instruction.
Sekhmet living Goddess of Life,
fearsome in your wrath, wondrous in your mercy,
changeable and wondrous as the winds.
Truly you are
the Divine Physician, the awe-inspiring healer,
and upon me, have taken pity.
I thank you,
Great Lady, Lioness of Two Lands.
Goddess for all time.
Teacher of those who will listen."

CHAPTER SIXTEEN

SCORPION

MEDICINE AND MAGICK

"One of the most healing things you can do is recognize where in your life you are your own poison."

STEVE MARABOLI

Scorpions are nocturnal arachnids that have literally been on the planet for 400 million years, dating them older than the dinosaurs. These small but deadly predators can be found everywhere but Antarctica and New Zealand. There are over 1,750 species. While all scorpions are venomous, only 25 species have venom that is capable of killing a human. The US is home to only one dangerous species and that is the bark scorpion of Arizona.

Why Scorpions? They are resilient! They are champions of survival. Scorpions have amazing lungs called book lungs that allow them to survive submerged underwater for 48 hours. They can also live a year without food. They thrive in the harshest of environments. They also glow under ultraviolet light which is pretty impressive. Scorpions reach maturity in one to three years and live for about one to three years as adults, which means for an arachnid they live a surprisingly long time!

While it is completely understandable that one would have resistance connecting with scorpions through shapeshifting and totemism; it can also be quite inspiring and healing to activate through apprehension. By conquering one's fears one triumphs! Vincent Van Gogh once said, "What would life be if we had no courage to attempt anything?"

Looking back at how the ancient's feared and honored this spectacular creature, you can't help but feel some intrigue. In Egypt, scorpions were feared but also respected, amulets made in the shape of scorpions were said to protect one from the *evil eye*. African shamans used the venom of scorpions for medical purposes as a healing agent. In Mesopotamia, Ishhara was a Scorpion Goddess of Love and Mother of the Seven Sebuttu. An oath made to Ishhara was sacred. The Hindu's honored Chelamma, also a scorpion goddess. The Aztec's had Malinalxochitl, Goddess of Snakes, Scorpions and Insects. In Akkadian or early Mesopotamia, scorpion men guardians called "Aqrabuamelu" kept watch over the God Shamash.

In Greek mythology, Orion made a threat against all the animals of the world and Artemis, who was their protector, was not happy. So ,she sent a scorpion down to sting the great boasting Orion which resulted in his death. Some say that she dipped one of her arrows in scorpion venom regardless Zeus being so impressed made scorpion part of the constellations out of respect. Other myths credit Juno for being the one who disliked Orion's boasting and arrogance so she placed a scorpion on one of his hunting paths and it stung him, killing him. Both Orion and Scorpio have constellations, both being mighty, but you will notice they are on opposite sides and never seen in the sky together.

Most assume scorpions to be negative omens of death, pain and vengeance. Even those born under the zodiac sign scorpio have a reputation of being fierce and cruel; they basically come with a warning. In this chaos, fear and state of the world we are living in, calling upon scorpion can only increase one's abilities of being resilient; self reliant and seeing where as individuals we have consumed or created toxins in our lives that are ready to be dealt with. Scorpion energy can be transforming but oftentimes it will trigger self criticism and deep shadow work.

You can read countless books and articles on embracing scorpion as a totem or spiritual messenger. Ultimately the connection you make with any *being* is yours to define and activate. No two people will have the same experience with any totem or animal through shapeshifting, just like no two people will have the same energetic connection with a particular deity that one is called to embrace. It is vital to honor the individual and avoid making comparisons or stepping into the ego brain of doubts and insecurities.

As part of your observation with scorpion it is helpful to read such articles but remember that this is your connection and it is highly suggested that you observe visually before you embrace other people's connection or insight on any animal or deity.

With scorpion, you may not be a nocturnal creature and have access to them in your own yard. So youtube or documentary videos are great tools for observing. Watch how scorpion is both predator and, yes; prey. Every individual, deity, animal, insect...Every being is both predator and prey in very unique ways. That is why totemism and animism are vital tools in helping the individual embrace characteristics that are distinct to the shapeshifter. Caution: we have been taught to fear "creepy crawlies" especially scorpions. So ,when you watch the videos make sure you journal whether your discomfort is from your own fears and experiences or if it has been taught to you. This will also help as you step into the healing attributes of working with scorpion.

A big essence of scorpion energy is accepting those things about yourself that others may see or feel as a threat. Or those things about yourself that you yourself have learned to reject. Scorpio energy is all about revealing those aspects that you have kept guarded.

MEDITATION CONNECTION WITH SCORPION ENERGY

Go into a meditative state, quiet your mind and focus on your breath. Relax your physical body and allow yourself uninterrupted time to go within. See your physical body covered in armor, thick plates of armor, see yourself poised and ready to attack. You may be armed, or you may not. But simply allow yourself to connect with the part of you that is on guard, ready to react and attack, this is your predator aspect. Everyone has one and for now you are simply practicing allowance. Feel what your predator self feels like.

(Pause)

Make an observation of yourself.

Now see the armor being removed. Put down the weapons, pinchers or stinger and allow yourself to be exposed. Lift up the guards that you put up in defense and see what lies beneath the surface. This is your prey aspect. Everyone has one and for now you are simply stepping into observation. Feel your prey side.

(Pause)

Bring your awareness back to your breath and back to the present moment. Open your eyes and take out your journal. It's time to put into writing your observations of yourself.

- What are your defense mechanisms? How do you step into predator mode and why? List examples. In these times, was it absolutely necessary to step into predator role?
- What are you prey mechanisms? How do you allow yourself to be prey and why? List examples. In these times, was it absolutely necessary to become prey?

Surprisingly enough, there are many scorpion deities from many pantheons. To some they were the embodiment of evil, poison spewing gods. To others they were fierce defenders and guardians. The ancient civilizations of Babylon, India, Maya, Greece and Egypt all honored and were familiar with the scorpio constellation and its link to scorpion attributes.

Astrologically, the sign of the 8th House of Scorpio is represented by not just the scorpion but also the eagle and the phoenix. These animals all represent transformation, rising above to new heights and the ability to be reborn from the ashes. The zodiac scorpion is associated with sex, death, rebirth, psychic abilities and great strength.

As members of the arachnid (spider) family, the scorpion is known for its heightened sense of touch, not sight. They have underneath their last pair of legs comb-like structures which are their organs of touch which they rely upon more so than their two eyes that rest in the center of their head.

As a teacher, mentor, mirror and guide; scorpion energy activates a more meaningful method of touch, typically emotionally and spiritually. Those who have encountered a "scorpio" person born between October 23rd – November 22nd can attest to the fact that they were touched in an emotional, physical or spiritual manner. Those born under the sign of scorpio tend to be highly emotional, sexually charged and full of a passion that often misleads people to think they are fire signs when in fact they are a water sign ruled by their intuition and heavy at times with emotions. This is true when encountering a real scorpion. Typically stumbling upon a scorpion triggers a fear response. Not all that different from meeting a scorpio sign.

GODDESS SELKET

In Egypt, the Goddess of Fertility, Animals, Nature, Medicine, Magic and Healing was known as Selket, her other names being Serqet, Selqet, Serket and Selcis. Her name literally means "she who tightens the throat or she who causes the throat to breathe." Scorpion medicine and healing to the Egyptians often involved using the source of the poison to cure the one poisoned. For example, if one was stung by a scorpion the venom of the scorpion was used to heal. Think of the saying "hair of the dog that bit you." Or homeopathic healing which is based upon "like cures like" or the substance believed to cause the ailment just might also be the cure.

When working with the Goddess Selket, one of her main roles and duties was to magically protect and cure those who were bitten or stung. She was the Patroness of Magicians who dealt with venomous bites. Selket was depicted as a woman with a scorpion on her head. On other occasions she was depicted as a scorpion with the head of a woman. She was often associated with childbirth and nursing. She was referred to as Protector of the Embalmer's Tent.

While her family line is unknown, she has been linked to Horus as one of the watchers of his sons. It was thought that she was either the mother or daughter of Ra, who embodied the scorching desert heat of the sun. It was mentioned that Selket helped Isis hide young Horus from Set.

Her duties and titles consisted of but were not limited to: Goddess of Healing against poisons and venomous stings. Goddess of Protection, especially during childbirth. Patron of medical priests, doctors and physicians dealing with stings. Patron of Pharoahs. Funerary Goddess, she who was the guardian of Horus' "Kebehsenuef" son, who was responsible for the canopic jars containing the intestines. Protector of the Scorpion Kings of Early Egypt. Guardian of the Dead. She who demands the dead be remembered. She was known to sting the unrighteous. Goddess of Magic.

In Egypt, the scorpion was a symbol of chaos and some believed the restless dead would take on the physical form of scorpion. The Egyptians honored scorpion essence as a potent guardian for souls moving from one world to the next.

Call upon Selket when you are in need of healing from a "sharp tongue" or when someone has cast poisons your way, taking into consideration that you may very well be the one sending you poison. These poisons can be harsh words, deeds or negativity. Selket will help to pull out the toxins. She can help you open your throat chakra and begin to speak your truth and she can also close your throat chakra when you are in need of controlling the harmful words you speak. Selket as guardian is a goddess to call when you are in need of protection.

A statue of Selket was found standing guard at Tutankhamun's shrine, or his canopic chest. She was the guardian of his intestines. This statue shows a woman with a scorpion on her head with both arms outstretched. The hieroglyph on the lid states that Selket will put her arms upon what is inside of her outstretched arms.

RITUAL CONNECTION WITH SELKET

In calling upon Selket, take time to set your intent and focus on what it is you are in need of protection against or for. Remember that scorpion medicine is all about the power to change, transform and rebirth. Rebirthing can be an uncomfortable intent. Scorpion energy will provide strength, and promote self preservation. Scorpion will also help one to rid oneself of one's own poison. Also note that there are times where something must die in order for something else to live. Trust your instincts and Selket will help you to decipher when to strike and when not to.

Altar cloth: gold, red, yellow to represent the heat of the desert sun.

Gemstones: tourmaline, carnelian, labradorite, lapis lazuli, hematite.

Herbs: juniper berry, plantain, basil, sage, wormwood, nettle.
It should be noted that the herb plantain is an excellent plant to use when bitten or stung by an insect, simply chew or macerate the leaf and pack it

onto the bite site. Plantain is known for drawing out the toxins. Along with wormwood, which has a long history of being consumed to help eliminate one of internal parasites.

Season: fall and winter.

Chakras: throat and root.

Symbols: scorpion, ankh, scepter, red or gold candle.

Once you have set your altar and focused on your intention and desire to connect, cast your circle or create your container. Remembering to secure time and space where your ritual will not be interrupted. Once your circle is cast, call upon Selket in your own words. Light your red or gold candle and kneel or sit before the altar, moving into a comfortable position.

Begin by taking a deep inhale and exhale it out completely. Breathe in and breathe out. Allow each exhale to take you into a deep state of relaxation, just by focusing on your breath and clearing your mind of all outside thoughts. Breathe in 2... 3... 4... and out 2...3...4... (repeat 3 times).

Now using your mind's eye, I want you to see yourself standing in front of a large golden pyramid. Feel the desert sands of Egypt under your feet. Take a few deep breaths here and adjust to the dry atmosphere. When you are steady, looking in front of you there is a doorway that leads down underneath this large pyramid. It is very dark but you feel a pull to enter.

Slowly and cautiously, for it is very dark and while there may be lanterns, they only give off a faint light. It is very quiet in this passageway beneath the pyramid and the dirt is cold beneath your feet. But you can't resist moving forward.

The passageway seems to slope downward, taking you deeper and deeper. As you approach each lantern, you give thanks for the small flickers of light. The passageway begins to open up and you find yourself inside a large room. It is not ornate but rather dull. There are sandstone walls and it is much lighter in this room with the addition of numerous lanterns. There is a thick layer of dirt on the ground and your feet can't help but sink down into the cold but dry sand. You notice an altar set up in the middle of the room and it is crawling with scorpions; they seem to be moving in a spiral pattern on the altar. Making their way around sacred tools and being very respectful as they move, so as to not move or shift the objects on the table.

Behind the altar stands a woman completely dressed in gold with long flowing sleeves and on her head sits a very large scorpion head dress. You

EGYPTIAN ANIMALS AS GODS

have discovered the sacred preparation room of Selket the Goddess of Magick and Scorpions. It is she who prepares the dead for their trip into the underworld. This room is the first stop on their journey.

You are not dead, but there are parts of you that do need to die in order to allow you to move forward on this journey. Selket is here to help you. She motions you to approach the altar where she meets you.

She picks up a sage bundle and lights it using one of the candles on the altar. She asks you, "Are you ready to be cleared from toxic self loathing?" Once you respond she smudges you, slowly and efficiently. She completely surrounds you with sacred, cleansing smoke. She then places the smudge back into its dish on the altar and picks up a chalice made of alabaster with a lotus engraved upon it. She asks you if are you ready to be washed clean of all the poisons you have swallowed that have created blockages in your life? Once you answer, she dips her fingers into the chalice and begins to anoint you, first on your crown chakra, then your third eye. Your throat chakra she spends more time on before moving to your heart chakra, solar plexus chakra, sacral chakra and your root chakra being last.

Once you have been anointed, she places the lotus chalice back onto the altar. She looks at you intently and her eyes, though piercing, have a calming motherly gaze. She picks up one of the scorpions crawling on the altar and asks you to hold out your hand.

Scorpions can be intimidating, she says, but so can life. There are moments of pain and pleasure, growth itself can sting. She places the scorpion into your hand. She reminds you that scorpions are powerful transformers and they come with a caution. "Pick and choose your battles in life, know when to sting and when to retreat, there is balance in all things and you must strive to seek that. For without balance, foundations crumble. Hold onto your truth, don't swallow the poisons that are projected onto you by those who are weak and wish to destroy your strength. Rise up! You are confident and demand respect just like this scorpion in your hand. You don't have to sting to be respected."

Give Selket gratitude for her blessing, and this reminder. For that which is remembered lives. See the scorpion in your hand moving up to your wrist where it transforms itself into an intricate golden bracelet. A constant reminder of your inner strength and the power of your words.

Feel yourself turning away from the goddess and moving back towards the dark passageway, slowly returning to the daylight that awaits you outside of the pyramid. With each step you take, you feel yourself slowly coming back to the present. Feeling more confident, empowered and strong.

Taking a nice deep breath in and exhaling it out. Breathing deep into your diaphragm filling yourself up with oxygen. Exhale fully and breathe in and breathe out. Keep breathing at your own pace until you feel yourself fully back in the present moment. Slowly coming back to the room.

Meditation Response
Fall and winter are both considered the season of harvest and the season of death. They represent a time to rest and recuperate. Working with Selket during the season of scorpio particularly will promote a powerful self acceptance and self love. Selket will help one to gain strength to enter the shadow part of the year and give one the courage to face the changes necessary for the New Year approaching.

CATIVATING SCORPION THROUGH YOGA TECHNIQUES

The scorpion asana or yoga pose is very advanced and should not be attempted by everyone. So, for calling upon scorpion, utilizing a mudra is more easily accessible and can be done by everyone. A mudra is a hand gesture that is used during meditation to channel and direct the body's energy flow. There are hundreds of hand mudras that improve health and energy levels. In Sanskrit mudra means "seal" or "sign".

Each finger on the hand represents a different element. The thumb-fire, forefinger-air, middle finger-ether or spirit, ring finger-earth and the pinky finger-water. Working with the tips of the fingers allows one to tap into the nerves. Mudra practice complements any meditative practice as they positively impact on the brain.

Apana mudra: to assist mental and physical digesting as well as helping one eliminate waste material from the body. Emotionally and mentally this can be used to rid one of "evil" or "poison". This mudra improves digestion and strengthens the immune system on all levels. To do this, simply bring your second and third finger to your thumb, which allows your pinky and index finger to be extended. Hold this mudra whilst sitting in a comfortable cross legged position for three to eleven minutes. Giving gratitude to your body's ability to heal itself and remove toxins from your physical and mental body. This mudra physically can be compared to a scorpion with both front pincers extended.

Tarjani mudra: this mudra is made by holding the right hand vertically in front of the chest, with only the index finger raised while the other fingers and thumb make a clenched fist. The outer edge of the palm (the pinkie side) faces outward toward the view, while the thumb-side of the palm faces inward to the deity. This is a gesture of warning, or can be thought of as a hand sign of expelling demons or illusion.

Kashyapa mudra: if you want powerful protection from vampiric energy and people with negative attitudes, this is the mudra for you. This mudra acts as a guard fending off negative vibes. It creates balance and helps to keep one grounded.

Place the thumb underneath your forefinger and middle finger, let the thumb poke out and make a fist. This mudra is perfect if you are in a group and are wanting to protect yourself in a subtle way. The Kashyapa mudra also creates union between one's masculine and feminine side. It is very helpful when in conflict or amongst toxic people.

All mudras can be performed either when sitting or when engaging in walking meditations. Simply hold the pose and focus on your breath. Each mudra can be repeated throughout the day and held for as long as necessary. Some yogis will hold mudra poses for up to 40 minutes.

CHAPTER SEVENTEEN

SNAKE

MEDICINE AND MAGICK

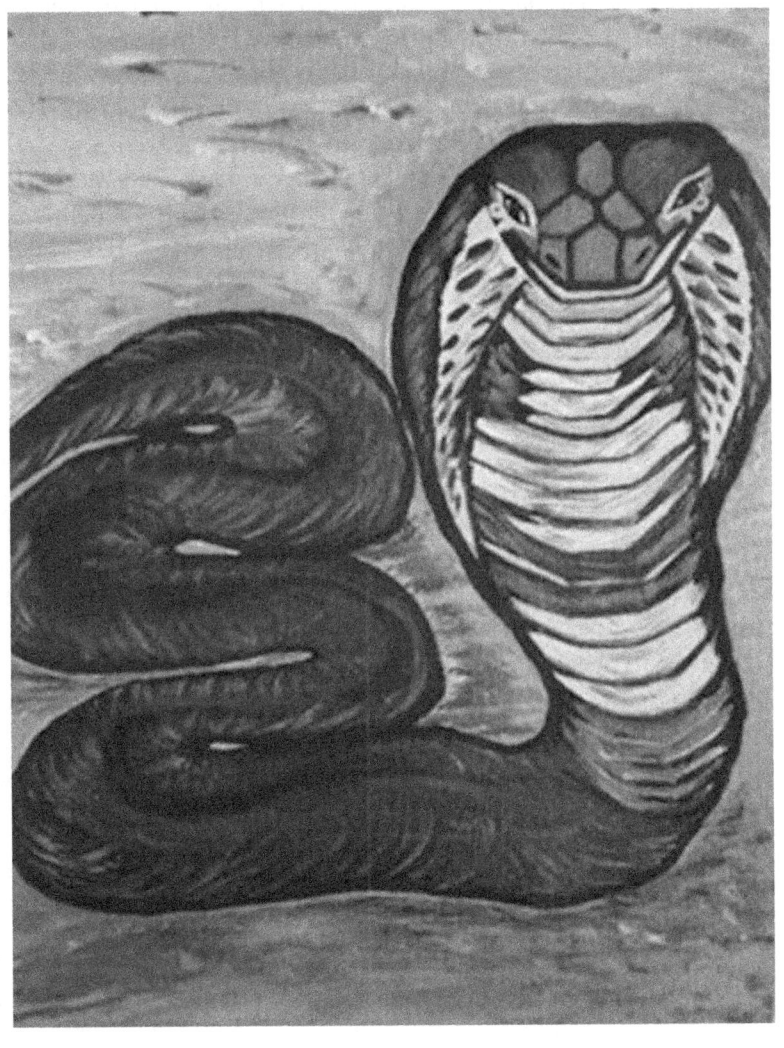

"Just as a snake sheds its skin, we must shed our past over and over again."

BUDDHA

One of the most venomous snakes in the world is the king cobra. Cobras can reach up to eighteen feet in length which also makes them one of the longest snakes in the world. Cobras are mainly found in India, Southern China and Southeast Asia.

These large and powerful snakes are now listed as "vulnerable" since 2010; this is due to their habitats being destroyed. They too have fallen prey to human's need to expand and they are poached for their meat, skin and medicinal values, which are used often in traditional Chinese medicines. In India, killing a cobra comes with a prison sentence of up to six years as they have been on the Wildlife Protective Act since 1972. Cobras are also protected in Vietnam under the Cobra Conservancy, which is an education source for the public to better understand and protect the cobras. Through this program, cobras are actually micro-chipped and monitored. This is all part of a movement to reduce illegal wildlife trade.

Cobras have a nasty reputation but are very rarely seen as they prefer the shadows and avoid humans. These snakes are not known as being aggressive unless provoked or their safety threatened. Cobras hunt during the day and have an amazing ability to unhinge their jaws to allow them to swallow prey that is much larger than their head. Snakes possess an organ inside the roof of their mouth that gives them an intense sensory receptor. Once the scent of prey is picked up, they use their forked tongue to locate the source. They also feel the vibrations through their body and can detect prey up to 300 feet away. Cobras primarily prey upon other snakes, lizards and rodents. Cobras are the only snakes to be nest builders, which are constructed by the males and intensely watched over until the eggs hatch.

Known throughout history in many different myths and legends, snakes have been regarded as sacred symbols of healing, transformation, fertility and immortality. This superpower of immortality is due to their ability to shed and slough off their dead skin and appear to be reborn or reincarnated from themselves. This ability to shed is not only something snakes do – ALL animals shed. As mammals we humans shed too! Reptiles actually only shed periodically and their skin comes off in one piece. This is a process of molting and sloughing called *ecdysis*.

Snakes shed skin to clear off bacteria and parasites when they are growing. Unlike our skin, a snake's skin does not grow with the snake. Eventually they have to shed a layer in order to grow. Snakes typically will enter water when they are ready for a shed, then they will cause a rip in this old layer of skin and slither, sometimes rubbing against rocks or branches, to help loosen the dead skin off, leaving behind a complete inside-out snake shed that typically has parasites and bacteria attached to it.

Snakes move or rather glide in a wave-like motion by using their underbelly scales to push backwards. This movement is referred to as undulation, which some may know as being a movement in belly dancing. Serpentine movement is one of the three main techniques in belly dance or Middle Eastern Dance. This style of dancing is not a sexual enticement but rather a celebration of the body and the sacred divine feminine. The snake is known throughout other cultures as a symbol of the goddess.

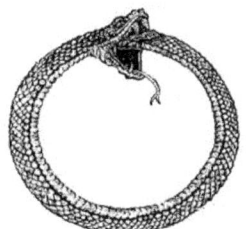

OUROBOROS

This powerful symbol of a snake/serpent eating its own tail, at times portrayed as a dragon consuming its own tail, is a symbol of wholeness, infinity, rebirth and transformation. The ouroboros originated in ancient Egypt in the "Enigmatic Book of the Netherworld" which was a funerary text found in the tomb of Tutankhamun. The ouroboros is shown twice in this book and scholars believe it to represent the beginning and the end. The ouroboros was later adopted by western traditions through the Greeks. The name stems from the Greek root *oura* – meaning *tail* and *boros* – meaning *eating*. It is well known throughout Gnosticism, Hermeticism and alchemy practices.

Alchemist scholars have embraced the ouroboros as a symbol of integration, assimilation of the opposite and symbol of immortality. The ability to consume one's self or "devouring oneself and turning oneself into a circulatory process." Carl Jung honored the ouroboros as a mandala of alchemy. A mandala which depicts the wholeness of life itself. Many cultures embrace mandalas in their teachings, including Christianity. At the center of a mandala, the focal point is typically always a circle; it draws you in and begs you to question what is at your center?

Even in Norse mythology, we know that one of Loki's children is Jormungandr, an incredibly large serpent that lives in the ocean. Jormungandr is so large that he can encircle the earth and grasp his own tail between his teeth.

The shape or symbol of a circle we know to mean containment and boundaries. Which is why magic or spell work is often done within the safe confines of an energetic or physically crafted circle. The circle also represents time, continuity, completion, never ending and whole unto itself.

In the text "The Chrysopeia of Cleopatra" an early alchemical text, you can find a depiction of the ouroboros and within are the words *hen to pan* which translates as "one is the all." In the western traditions, the ouroboros has been adopted as the yin-yang symbol, which represents duality and the cycle of all things, soul and body, the two opposites together meaning "one which is all."

Witches call upon this ancient symbol for it is a reminder of the cycle of life, unity, wholeness unto oneself, the Law of Karma, primordial unity and the power of transformation.

Carl Jung wrote, "The ouroboros is a dramatic symbol for the integration and assimilation of the opposite, of the shadow. This feedback process is at the same time a symbol of immortality, since it is said of the ouroboros that he slays himself and brings himself to life, fertilizes himself and gives birth to himself. He symbolizes the One, who precedes the clash of opposites, and he therefore constitutes the secret of the prima materia which unquestionably stems from man's unconsciousness."

KUNDALINI

Known as primordial energy or serpent power, Kundalini is life force, spiritual energy that everyone possesses but oftentimes lies dormant and coiled around the muladhara chakra which most know as the root chakra. Kundalini is a Sanskrit word which means "coiled up". Tantra yoga Kundalini is an aspect of "Shakti" or divine feminine energy. This energy is within all of us, just waiting to be awakened through expansion.

It is believed that in order to achieve liberation and/or Nirvana, one must embrace and awaken Kundalini energy. Not only does Kundalini create Nirvana but overall it brings about feelings of euphoria, bliss, enlightenment, an awakened sense of smell, sight and taste.

"The serpent energy located at the base of one's spine is the anchor to the individual's duality. Just like the archetypical "Eve" we are unable to grow and transform without listening to the wisdom of the "Serpent". The practice of Kundalini yoga and meditation are utilized to facilitate that opening and flow by systematically releasing the tension and emotional blocks that keep us from being fully alive. With the use of mantra, pranayama, mudra, kirya and meditation, the practice of Kundalini awakens knowledge of self and connection to the essence for the divine in all life. The awakened Kundalini is nurtured as it is allowed to rise up through the body." – Ami Porter, Kundalini yogi.

Another way this was described to me when I began my yoga practice some eighteen years ago was: at the base of our spine lie two snakes, one depicted as white and one depicted as black. As one raises this snake-like serpentine energy throughout the spine, the lifeline of the body, these two snakes begin to coil and move up the spine where they finally rest head upon head upon head creating a crown on top of the crown chakra. Here it rests in a state of unity, conscious expansion and one's creative potential has been unleashed.

"Kundalini energy is the mother energy she is like a sweet dance of ecstasy rising like the cobra; she is the vessel from which the goddess awakens. She allows us to experience greater states of bliss and all sensual aspects of life. Through the practice of meditation, kriya and breathing, we are able to awaken Kundalini and integrate it into our daily lives so we can live to the fullest potential." – Annmarie Brown.

Are you ready to tap into your Kundalini with the help of the divine Mother Cobra? Kundalini is both a path and the goal. It is both the foundation and the practice.

EMBRACING COBRA THROUGH MOVEMENT

Kundalini yoga is often called the "Mother of all yogas" anyone can do Kundalini just like anyone can do yoga. That is the beauty with yoga is you are the one that moves your body. There are correct ways to hold each pose or asana but that is determined by your physical body and personal limits. The practice is in the doing. For this activation you will be using cobra pose and meditation to connect and feel the cobra energy within rising.

Step by step into cobra (Bhujangasana) pose:

- Move onto your stomach.
- Place your forehead down, feet extended and hands by your chest, elbows bent.

- Take a nice deep inhale and, as you stretch, push your hands down, lifting your chest and upper body off the ground. Exhale and let your head lift up and look forward, stretching your neck. It is important to let your shoulders drop away from your ears.
- Push your hands into the ground; keep your legs extended with tops of your feet resting on the ground.
- Focus on your breath, nice and slow. If this is uncomfortable for your neck, then bring your head to your chest or let it simply rest hanging down. Breathe into your diaphragm.

Now it's time to combine visualization with movement. From here, simply bring your forehead to the ground and rest your body. Allow your arms to rest by your side with hands beside your chest. Close your eyes and bring your awareness to your breath. Take a slow deep inhale and exhale. Breathe in the count of four and out to the count of four. Continue this breath cycle until your mind is clear and your physical body is relaxed.

In this state you are ready to bring your attention and focus to your tailbone or root chakra. Send your inhale down to this area and allow yourself to feel a tingling sensation. Picture in your mind a snake within, coiled around your root chakra. The more you picture this snake, the stronger the tingling sensation becomes. The stronger this tingling sensation becomes, the more the snake begins to slowly uncoil. Feel as the snake begins to unwind and slither up your spine in a slow, precise, wave-like motion. Moving back and forth, back and forth, back and forth, up your spine. Allow your hands to push up off the ground and bring your upper body up off the floor or mat. When this snake reaches your neck, the snake begins to become wider and you may feel that its head is opening up like a cobra to expand over the base of your neck and head. Take a deep breath in and exhale fully. With your eyes closed, bring your back, head and neck up, allowing the cobra to fully open up with you. When you are ready, bring your head down to a forward position and open your eyes. Allow yourself to feel the cobra's head resting upon your own and feel its eyes connecting with your sight as you both gaze forward.

Cobra pose is very good for increasing flexibility in your spine which is your life line. It helps regulate the digestive system, tones abdominal muscles and helps bring your chakras and energy points into a balanced state.

If you focus on snake energy, you will know and activate your abdominal muscles more which will help you maintain a proper posture. Snakes rely upon the strength of their abdomen muscles to move.

This pose also opens up your heart space, lungs and allows you to breathe in life a bit easier. It is very beneficial for activating the optical nerve and raising your conscious sight. It is recommended that you hold this pose for up to fifteen seconds and then release, repeating this pattern for up to seven minutes.

SNAKE PRIESTESSES

Many cultures have honored and worshipped the snake as divine and sentient. Many are familiar with the Minoan Snake Goddess statue which depicts a bare breasted woman holding a snake in each hand. In Myanmar, a Burmese priestess must kiss a king cobra upon the head three times as part of a fertility ritual. The Goddess Inanna was believed to have snake priestesses dressed in deep scarlet colored robes.

Myanmar has a temple called the Hmwe Paya or "Snake Pagoda" dedicated to snakes and within it are numerous pythons lying about the temple. Each year thousands make pilgrimages to this temple to make offerings, to pray and hope that the snakes will assist their prayers in being answered. This pagoda or temple was founded in 1974 by a Buddhist monk who was tending the old pagoda. Inside, the monk found two large pythons wrapped around a statue of Buddha. The monk dutifully carried the snakes out to the jungle and returned to clean the pagoda. Within a day the snakes were back, and a third had joined. Each time, the monks would carry the snakes out to the jungle, and each time they would return. Eventually the monks came to see the snakes as holy, possibly the reincarnated souls of monks who used to tend to the pagoda. The monks stopped removing the snakes and instead began taking care of them.

Even in our modern world, the snake is still embraced through dance and meditations which include holding or allowing snakes to slither over your body. There are even massage clinics that have one lie down on the massage table and allow snakes to slither all over you, giving you an overall healing serpent massage.

By definition of priestess, it is one of service and devotion. These snake or serpent priestesses are embracing the history of our ancestors and are now offering sacred rituals, dance and workshops where snakes are offered to guests to assist the attendees in healing through the mystical power of the snake.

The Hopi tribes of Arizona believe that their ancestors came from the underworld and each year they pray for rain in a ceremony called the snake dance.

WADJET – THE COBRA GODDESS OF EGYPT

Depicted as a snake-headed woman, or a snake with a woman's head, woman with two snake heads and often as a cobra, Wadjet was honored as the Patron Goddess and Protector of Lower Egypt. She was linked with the Nile Delta region and associated with the world of the living. She was often thought of as a protective deity to the pharaohs.

In her form of cobra she was poised and ready to strike. In another depiction she was shown to be coiled up sitting upon the head of Ra. She was worshipped in her temple at the ancient Imet in the Nile Delta as the "Lady of Imet."

"The Goddess Wadjet appears in the form of the living uraeus to anoint your head with her flames. She rises up on the left side of your head and she shines from the right side of your temples without speech; she rises up on your head during each and every hour of the day, even as she does for her father Ra, and through her the terror which you inspire in the spirits is increased... She will never leave you, is of you and strikes into the souls which are made perfect."

THE BOOK OF THE DEAD

Wadjet, also Buto, Uto or Edjo, was known throughout myths as the nurse to the God Horus. She kept Isis safe from Seth and helped her find refuge in the delta swamps. She was titled the "Eye of Ra" and the symbol that we know as the Eye of Ra is oftentimes referred to as the Wadjet. It was in this form that she would avenge her father and cause the destruction of mankind.

Wadjet's sister Nekhbet was seen as more of a gentle, nurturing goddess while Wadjet was very aggressive and thought to have similar qualities to Sehkmet. Some interchange the myths and believe it was Wadjet whose anger was slumbered with trickery with beer dyed red to resemble blood, just like Sehkmet was. Or were they one and the same? Wadjet and her sister were both protectors and depicted on the queen's headdresses in the Eighteenth Dynasty with two snakes; one for each sister. Wadjet was also linked with the Vulture Goddess and some scholars believe the Vulture Goddess to be another aspect of Wadjet.

Some of Wadjet's titles include but are certainly not limited to: "Great Serpent, She of the Fiery Eyed Cobra, Lady of Devouring Flame, Noble Serpent Who Flowed Forth From The Eye, The Wadjet Eye, Serpent Mother, Protector of Horus, She Who Brings Truth and Justice, Mistress of Fear, Goddess of the

Placenta, Lady of Spells, Mother of Creation, Queen of the Gods, She Who Loves Silence, The Eye."

THE WADJET

The Wadjet Eye, an ancient symbol most commonly referred to as the "Eye of Horus" is a symbol of protection, royal power, good health and is used to ward off evil. The eye is the most popular of all the amulets and symbols of ancient Egypt. The Wadjet Eye has been used and is still used in magical ceremonies and as a sigil to restore balance, offer protection and healing. In my home, there is a Wadjet right beside the front door. It is charged and blessed to protect and watch over everyone within my home.

With the Goddess Wadjet being one who protects and watches over children, birthing mothers, pharaohs, kings and the people, it is no surprise that the ancient Egyptians would call upon her watchful protection with the inscription or depiction of her *eye*. She was a Goddess of the Living, so naturally she would be called upon to protect and watch over the living.

We can sum it all up with cobras and the ancient Goddess Wadjet as being divine sources of protection. Cobras are the only snakes in the entire world that build nests and watch over and protect their eggs.

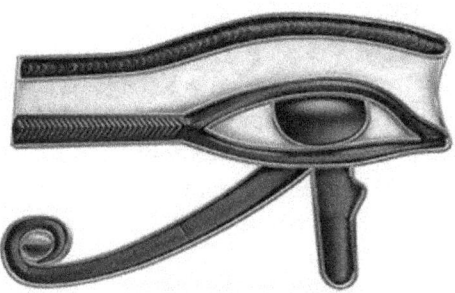

The following is a protection spell for your home and family. It is important with spell work that you are specific. What kind of protection are you in need of? While most are familiar with the sigil of the evil eye and how it protects one from jealousy, when working with Wadjet in spell or ritual format, the more specific you can be, the better. For example, one may call upon protection from gossip, unwanted visitors, solicitors, or those who have bad intentions. Another may call upon protection from the elements, while another may call upon protection of their children or animals. The intention of protection is very broad and for spell work to really be effective; the more details, the better. Be clear with your words. After all, the very words we speak create the reality around us.

RITUAL TO CALL UPON WADJET FOR PROTECTION

We are living in crazy times! The world has gone topsy-turvy and who knows what the truth is and who the real threat is? Protection spells, rituals and ceremonies are not a New Age concept. It is our instinctual fight mode that causes us to want to protect and provide for ourselves and our families. This is nothing new or modern. The below ritual contains the ingredients for making a "witch's bottle". These spell bottles have been crafted and used for centuries. They were made and then buried on the owner's property to ensure protection.

For the witch's bottle you will need the following items:

- empty jar with a lid – any size and shape.
- protection herbs – thyme, sage, palo santo.
- protection stones – black tourmaline, obsidian, blood stone.
- small pieces of paper and a pen to write with.
- items that represent protection to you – for example, I use porcupine quills.
- liquid to hold together – blessed water, blessed wine, urine, or even a tea made from the herbs above. The key is to allow the water to bind and allow the protection magic to flow.
- an image of the Wadjet Eye, Wadjet Goddess, snake figurine.
- candle – whatever color you choose.
- bonus ingredients – snake skin (if you have a snake in your home who has gifted you a shedding), hair from your home guardians (dogs or cats). Please do not pull the hair off!

CREATING YOUR CONTAINER FOR YOUR RITUAL

Please make sure you have a space close to the center of your home where you will be undisturbed. For this ritual, you will not need a formal altar dedicated to your intention of creating protection. A table with all your witch's bottle ingredients will serve as your altar.

Set the intention: what, who and for whom are you wanting protection from and/or for?

Clear your space: using either sacred smoke from a smudge bundle, incense stick or loose incense burning on a charcoal disc.

Call to the directions: welcome the ancestors and elements from the east, south, west and north

Invoke Wadjet: call to the Snake Goddess, Serpent Mother, Cobra Queen in whichever way you choose or you can use the invocation provided. Pick up your candle and illuminate your intention (light the candle) of calling upon Wadjet for protection and to assist you in crafting your witch's bottle.

Crafting your witch's bottle: offer the ingredients to the goddess and ask for her to charge, bless and bestow them with her protective energy and attributes.

"Goddess Wadjet, please guard and protect

(state the names, home and property you are wanting to be protected – be very descriptive) *infuse this* _____ (item) *with your venom that any who would do harm to* (state the names, home and property you are wanting to be protected)

will feel the poison in your bite and stay away, change direction and withdraw their intent to inflict harm, ill will or send negativity."

(place the item in the jar) continue this until all items have been blessed and charged with Wadjet's energy and essence. Once all items have been placed inside, pour your liquid over them.

"Goddess Wadjet, please guard and protect and infuse these items with this sacred liquid that it may bind this intent and create protection to

(state the names, home and property you are wanting to be protected)

bless them with your watchful eye and seal this magick for all time"

(write, draw or paint the Wadjet Eye on the lid of your jar)

*Optional – sprinkle with mint for an abundance of protection.

Sealing in the magick: with your witch's bottle crafted, blessed and sealed, you can place it on the center of your table next to your candle. Spend some time here. It may be helpful to go into a meditative state and really see within your mind how the people and places are being protected, what does that look like? What additional follow through steps do you need to do to ensure that they are protected? What does that look like?

By visualizing the intent and the spell and witch's bottle working, you absorb this into your subconscious, making it your new reality. Now what does it feel like to be protected? To know that you and your home and loved ones are being watched over? Allow yourself some time here to move through this way of visualizing the absorption of your magick.

Gratitude: in your own words and your own way; offer gratitude to Wadjet for her presence, her protection. Then offer gratitude to the ancestors and elemental assistants from each direction the north, west, south and east.

Burying your witch's bottle: in completion to your ritual, bury your jar either under your porch, at your gateway or entrance to your property. You can also place the jar by your doorway, inside or any other location you deem fitting. This is your magic after all, and your spell. Only you should know the location of your witch's bottle, unless of course you have crafted this with your family, which is another option.

Additional protective objects that you may want to add to your witch's bottle include:

Protective herbs: garlic, cinnamon, rosemary, cactus, ginger, allspice, star anise, mugwort, bay leaves, elderberries, mistletoe, yarrow, plantain, orange and lemon peels, pepper.

Protective stones: smoky quartz, obsidian, rainbow fluorite, blue kyanite, apache tear. Black tourmaline is really the best when it comes to protection. It repels and pushes away negativity. Tourmaline is extremely useful in deflecting any negative energy and intent! You can wear it, place it beside your computer, tuck it in your car, under your bed or keep it in your pocket. Blood stone is another good one and they are fairly small. One thing I have done in the past is to place one piece of blood stone in the main four corners of my home to offer protection.

Protective items: porcupine quills, cactus spines (spikes), thorns, rusty nails, iron pieces, barbed wire, needles, thumbtacks, anything with a sharp point to it.

BONUS ACTIVATION MEDITATION WITH WADJET

Find yourself a comfortable sitting position somewhere close to the center of your home. Allow your eyelids to gently close as you bring your focus and awareness to your breath. Inhale and exhale to the count of four and, with each breath cycle, give your physical body permission to relax.

Here in this state of relaxation, physically and mentally call upon Wadjet. You can do this by softly saying her name over and over again, either out loud or silently to yourself. Feel as her energy begins to slither around you, it may feel small like she is gliding gently around your legs as you sit. Or it may feel large with some pressure as she pushes against you. Allow her to move around you, coiling as she goes, around and around.

You may even feel your hips beginning to move in a circular motion as her energy begins to glide up near your tailbone. Here you begin to feel a tingle, almost a heat like tickle as she begins to glide side by side up your spine, coiling around your neck and resting her large cobra head on top of your head. Here she sits and with each exhale and inhale you feel her pushing against you. You begin to feel your inhale and exhale pushing against her, allow this exchange until you both sync the rhythm of your breaths together inhaling and exhaling.

Feel the calm begin to enter your body from the top of your head all the way down to your feet. Cobra energy is silent and gentle but very protective. Allow her to hold you and breathe into you her strength and protection.
(Pause for as long you would like)
Now bring your awareness back to your breath and this present moment, time and space. Allow Wadjet to glide back down your spine and uncoil herself and watch as she slithers away.

Journal your meditation experience.

BONUS PROTECTION MEDITATION WITH WADJET

Go into your meditative state. Allow yourself to physically relax and let go of any stresses, worries or tension. Give yourself permission to be at one with your surroundings. Settle in and focus your mind on your house. See your house as if you are looking at it from the street or yard. Think of all the wonderful things that your house provides you with and how grateful you are. Call upon Wadjet by saying her name out loud or silently to yourself. Repeat her name over and over again until you begin to feel a shift in the energy around you. She slithers in slowly with precision and begins to circle your house. The more she slithers the larger she becomes.

Watch as she coils around your home, encircling the entire outside over and over until her coils reach up to the roof. Here she slithers her head up onto your roof and her eyes meet yours. As she stares at you, her head expands and opens up so large it covers your entire roof. She has become your roof. Her eyes are piercing as she stares into you, almost as if she is asking you what you want from her.

Wadjet the Great Serpent Queen has completely coiled herself around your home and has created a shield of protection for your home and all who enter. Now you can ask of her exactly how she can continue to offer protection. Be specific.

Once you have spoken to her, offer her gratitude and watch as she begins to slither back down from your roof. With each uncoil she becomes smaller and smaller until soon she is the size of a small branch. Watch as she quickly slithers away out of sight.

As you gaze back at your home, it seems to vibrate with her residual protective energy. In the windows of your home you may even see her sacred symbol of the Wadjet glowing, creating a sigil; a reminder that your home is now guarded by the Great Goddess.

Journal your meditation experience.

For additional Wadjet protection magick you can draw or paint a Wadjet Eye near your entryway into your home. You can make this as noticeable as you wish. Or you can make it discreet. You can also have an image of a snake or even a snake figurine that can serve as a reminder of Wadjet and the protection she offers those who ask for it.

There are many runes, sigils and other symbols that you can draw, paint, inscribe that are great for protection magick. I highly recommended the following books to assist you on your journey into crafting and brewing up your own protection formulas:

- Sigil Witchery by Laura Tempest Zakroff.
- Practical Protection Magick by Ellen Dugan.

Native American Animals as Gods

CHAPTER EIGHTEEN

GRANDMOTHER SPIDER

MEDICINE AND MAGICK

"My life is a web of endless possibilities."

KATELYN PAULS

Spiders are carnivorous arachnids, which is a class of arthropods that also includes mites, ticks and scorpions. There are over 45,000 species of spiders living on every continent except Antartica. They have eight legs, two of which serve as antennae that they use to sense objects nearby.

Most people that I know have some kind of fear or apprehension when it comes to spiders, while others like myself are fascinated by them. Granted, I tend to steer clear of ones that I know to be poisonous, but for the most part I am known for either naming them or taking them outside if they are found inside my home.

Spiders are quite fascinating when you take the time to get to know them, observe them and learn some of the myths and legends surrounding them; which is my intent with this chapter. Spiders have eight legs and eight eyes. In numerology the number eight is all about career, finances, authority and business. It is also known as the equalizer, a cataclysmic force that can shape things, break things or create things. Think of karma, what you send out comes back, right? Well this essence of eight can coincide with spiders as they too are known for their attributes of hard work, practicality and intelligence.

Spiders are amazing! The ability they have to spin silk form their abdomen and use it to create masterpieces of art makes them captivating. Some spiders can live underwater, like the diving bell spider. They can fly over hundreds of miles or rather float using their delicate strands of silk to catch the breeze and parachute from one place to another. They can also dance, as you can observe in the peacock spider which, if you look at the attributes of a peacock, then you can see why this particular spider is known for strutting his stuff in an effort to entice the female spiders in a dance of courtship.

Still not a fan? That's okay. Arachnophobia is more than just a movie that came out in 1990 starring John Goodman; it is a real phobia that affects about five percent of the world population. But the fear of spiders has to have come from somewhere. Some psychologists believe that arachnophobia is based on cultural beliefs rather than the actual nature of spiders. A fear that was taught to us.

Who taught you to be cautious of spiders and why? What if instead of sharing fear, there was shared information? Is it too late to help the future generation avoid this fear of spiders? As a grandparent who lives in the desert of Southern Utah, we have our fair share of spiders, both in the home and out in the garden. My goal has been to take the time to teach by example and communicate honestly about all insects. Honestly, some I like and some I am not quite so fond of. However, it is important that I do my best to provide a safe environment for my granddaughter to develop her own relationship with the creepy crawlies, not encourage her to believe everything that I believe. Case in point; when we came upon a beetle in the garden, I picked it up and showed it to her and she was not too thrilled at the idea of it coming near her. Maybe we aren't completely programmed to fear spiders and other insects because of our elder's maybe it is something instinctual.

If you have ever seen a cat play with a moth, you can vouch for this. They have an instinctual desire to attack this flying insect, sometimes out of fun and sometimes for a snack. One reason we do not like poisonous spiders in our home or near our home is because of the animals we have and their instinctual desire to protect and defend their territory, no matter how small.

When we focus on the attributes of spiders and their ability to spin their homes from silken threads, we can at least have some appreciation and awe for the artwork that such a tiny creature can create.

Spiders transform liquid silk made from special glands within their abdomen that they spin into solid threads. They physically pull the silk from their silk secreting organs called spinnerets. The secret ingredient to web spinning is air current. The spider lifts the silk thread into the air which carries it from one physical anchor to another. Think of a web in between two branches.

Spiders, believe it or not, have been observed, honored and admired in many different pantheons. The Druids saw the spider as The Bard, The Ovate and The Druid. The spider is the guardian of ancient languages and alphabets. The spider's web holds the Ogham which is an Old Welsh, Pictish, Irish and Latin ancient primitive alphabet dating from the 6th – 9th century AD. The Ogham is the earliest form of writing found in Ireland. In some Native American traditions it was spider who was said to have woven the written alphabet giving mankind a way to record their history.

A spider's web is a spider's home, their source for storing food, catching food, holding and incubating their eggs, just to name a few uses. The spider weaves all that they need for survival. This ability to create and craft makes the essence and attributes of spider quite appealing and something to admire and aspire to implement.

The web itself is typically rebuilt every day. There is rhyme and reason to the design and, while most think that the web catches prey which unsuspectingly stumble into it as a trap, they are actually enticed by the intricate design of the web. The spider lures its prey into its web with its artistic abilities.

THE SACRED SPIRAL WITHIN THE WEB

Some of you may be mathematicians and can delve deeply into the mystery and qualities of the logarithmic spiral and the Fibonacci sequence. These logarithmic spirals appear all over in Nature from plants, galaxies, sea shells, weather patterns, our DNA molecules, our fingertips and spider webs, to name a few. These spirals exist because of the "principle of parsimony – a scientific principle which says that things are connected or behave in the simplest or most economical way. By maintaining the same shape through each successive turn of the spiral, the least amount of energy is used. In Nature, plants may grow in spirals so that leaves don't block the sun from older leaves or so that the maximum amount of rain reaches the roots." Embedded in this language of spirals is the language of mathematics.

Spiral magic or spiral medicine oftentimes refers to moments of deep personal growth beginning in the center and then moving outwards. In a spiral there are two ways to maneuver, one either spirals from the outside moving to deep into the center of their subconscious, shadow self, core of the issue and works on this inward essence for a bit. Or one begins from this center of depth and spirals out. Either way, spiral work is constant and always flowing. Think of a wave in motion; it is always moving, sometimes the wave is so small you can't really see the spiral, but it is there. In this state one is always progressing which is why you most likely have heard the saying "all things in life move in a spiral," or the quote by Barry H. Gillespie who said, "The path isn't a straight line; it's a spiral. You continually come back to things you thought you understood and see deeper truths." As humans we are constantly riding a spiral motion, whether we are aware of it or not. Growth does not occur by standing still or walking in a circle where one simply feels stuck and stagnant. We either enter the spiral and move back out or we stay in a place of stagnicity or denial. Robert Frost states it perfectly, "the best way out is always through." If you are uncomfortable, then move.

www.samwoolfe.com

SPIRALS EVERYWHERE

When a spider begins to weave its web, it begins in the center, strategically moving out. In the end the spider has built a very delicate and enticing work of art that attracts prey into its stickiness. At the end of the day the web is typically taken down just to be rebuilt again. How can we apply this to our lives? Each day we get up and weave together new opportunities for growth and expansion, to bring things to us or to send things away. We are constantly weaving our own web of living each day, just like the spider.

Years ago, I hosted a three day and three night women's empowerment gathering. Each of the sacred guides was asked to lead a workshop or ritual that centered on a different goddess. One guide selected "Grandmother Spider" in her ritual each guest participated in a weaving. We stood in a circle and a spool of yarn was passed around the circle, then we each took turns weaving yarn from one side to the other and slowly a web began to take shape. Unlike an actual spider's web that began in the center, this web began on the outside and together we wove into the center. Each woman who held the yarn and wove through the others weavings expressed what she wanted to weave into the world, in other words her intention. As a group we held the web intact while each guest took their turn. There were 30 guests in attendance and that was 30 intentions. The web at the end of the ritual was quite expansive. It was carefully taken down and folded and later thrown into a ritual fire to symbolize each intention being carried up and away into the cosmos.

Embracing Spider as teacher and messenger can be as simple as asking yourself; "what am I weaving today?" Each person on the planet today is a creator of their own day to day experience and overall outcome. You may not see yourself as an artist like a spider weaving an intricate mathematical equation into their web each day, but you are just that!

Journal prompt: what are you weaving today? Be specific!

Embodying Spider Through Movement
In yoga the spider pose is called Utkata Konasana or goddess pose.

Step by Step:

- Begin by standing tall with legs wide.
- Move into a forward bend with knees bent.
- Lift your heels so that you are standing on your toes.
- Cross your arms at the elbows and grasp your shins with the opposite hands.

Spider pose is a much dramatized goddess pose designed to open up the hips and groin. It is helpful for toning the core and strengthening the inner and outer thighs. Energetically it activates the root and sacral chakra.

Exercise: while moving into this pose, focus on your breath. Once you are comfortable in this position, close your eyes and visualize your body having the agility, strength and grace of spider. Hold this pose for 30–60 seconds then repeat.

CORD MAGICK

Just as a spider weaves silk into webs, humans too have been weaving fibers into cords for centuries. It could be safe to say that the early people looked to spiders for inspiration. We know that the practice of witchcraft mirrors Nature and that witches look to Nature for guidance, remedies and inspiration. When one activates connection with spider it is natural to want to weave. This can be achieved by braiding one's hair, knitting, weaving on a loom or crocheting. In witchcraft most are familiar with cord knotting. It is important to know that cord and knot workings are not limited to those who claim the responsibilities of living life as a witch. Knots are seen and honored in many pantheons and cultures.

In Rome oaths were taken by tying knots. Most are familiar with the "hand fasting" ceremony which stems from Scotland where a couple who choose to commit to each other in the presence of family, friends and a priestess or priest would bind their hands together with the cloth or cord that represents the clans in what we commonly refer to as "tying the knot." In Celtic mythology we see the Celtic knot work having sacred meaning and magical properties because they seem to flow without a beginning or an ending.

Even in Hindu practices, most are familiar with the necklaces referred to as "malas". These are meditative tools that help one to recite or count 108 mantras as part of their practice. Each mala is different and has its own unique properties which are determined by the beads or gemstones used, in between each bead or stone is a knot. While being worn the beads will each represent the chant or mantra with the wearer speaking that out loud or silently as they move their hands to each bead. The red string in Kabbalah is a symbol, sigil or talisman of protection when worn on the left wrist as a way of shielding one from negativity, misfortune and the evil eye.

When a potential member is initiated into a Coven, Grove or organized tradition the priest or priestess gifts them with a knotted cord to wear around their waist. This cord has different meanings and symbolism based upon the Coven and tradition being honored. When I was ordained by a Wiccan High Priestess, I was given a red cord measuring nine feet long to wear around my waist to represent the umbilical cord and the vow taken when initiated or ordained. When worn in ritual, ceremony or Coven space, the cord absorbs the energy of the event. When worn, the cord shows status, and serves as a reminder of the vows and promises made. The color of cords plays in as well, each color having its own meaning and symbolism. Some cords also contain a number of knots, with each knot representing a promise, vow or blessing. The wearing of a cord belt is personal and again often determined by what Wiccan tradition one is initiated into or one is embracing in a solitary practice.

CORD MAGICK EXERCISE

For this exercise you will need a cord of any length, color and texture. The intent is to create a tangible item charged for your own needs and purposes. The cord you choose will need to at least be able to be bound to your wrist. Selecting a texture or fiber that is not scratchy or would cause irritation is a bonus. When it comes to selecting your color of cord, I have found that it is best to go with a color that holds meaning to you. For example, red would be ideal if you are wanting to have more fire, passion and sexual confidence. Orange for confidence. Green for healing and abundance. Pink for love, self care and appreciation. Yellow for warmth, joy and to represent the sunshine. Just to list off a few.

After you have selected the cord you wish to work with, it's time to cleanse it. You can do this by soaking it in distilled water, blessed water or water with a pinch of sea salt or pink Himalayan salt. Next, let it dry. If you want to work with the lunar phases, you can take this cord outside and let it dry overnight underneath the light of the moon. Once your cord is dry you can then smudge it with sacred smoke. Again, remember that you can use incense, white sage, palo santo or my preferred is loose incense from plants that are grown on my property.

Now that your cord has been cleansed, you are ready to begin. With this exercise you do not need to cast a formal circle or create a ceremony or ritual. You can simply hold the cord within your hand and with your eyes closed focus on what this cord will mean to you. Why will you wear it? What will it symbolize to you? Breathe that intention and desire into your cord with each exhale, infusing it with life and purpose. If you feel called to, place a knot or two or visualize what each knot represents to you and then proceed. You may feel called to adorn your cord with inscriptions, sigils or beads. The key is that this is your weaving, your intention, and only you need to know what and why you wear this cord. There is never a need to explain to anyone.

Once complete, wrap it around your wrist. If you are wanting to receive with this intention then tie the cord onto your left hand, which represents your receptive side. If you are wanting to activate something then tie it onto your right hand, which represents your take action side.

Wear your cord night and day, never taking it off. When you magic is done and your cord magick complete, the cord will fall off on its own. If you are fortunate enough to have your cord fall off and you find it, you can take the pieces and bury them, burn them, place them as an offering at a sacred site that you are fond of, place them in the center of a labyrinth or place them on your altar as a reminder of the magick that your cord provided.

CORD MAGICK WITHIN A COVEN OR GROVE – USE THE RITUAL BELOW

The above exercise can be done within a Coven or Grove. Instead of using a single cord for each member you would use a spool of yarn or knitting cord. Collectively each guest would help to bless and charge and, while standing in a circle, the spool of yarn or cord would be passed around to each guest who would wrap it around their wrist, then pass it on to the next until there is a woven circle within the circle of guests. Once the inner circle has been woven then each member would take turns blessing or stating out loud their intention until the circle of woven blessings is complete. Then the cord would be cut between each member and then you would assist each other in tying the cord off. I have done this kind of magick in my Coven, Grove and at coming of age ceremonies. It is a beautiful reminder to look down at your wrist and remember all the supportive people you have in your life.

RITUAL ACTIVATION WITH GRANDMOTHER SPIDER

Altar prep: cloth with spiders or webs, directional candles in medicine wheel colors (air/yellow, fire/red, water/black, earth/white). Large spider in the center of the wheel. Yarn.

Ritual cleansing: smudge and water bless.

Welcome and intent: to honor and celebrate Grandmother Spider she who weaves the web of life, she who connects us all and anchors us in her web of deep ancestral knowledge.

Who are you? State this out loud.
I am _____ Today I am weaving the web of _____

Calling in the Medicine Wheel – Casting the Circle.
Hail and Welcome:
East – Sunrise, New Day, Eagle, Springtime
South – Fire, Heat of Afternoon, Summer, Wolf
West – Water, Dusk, Salmon, Autumn
North – Earth, Evening, Bear, Winter

Call to Grandmother Spider – She who weaves the web of life.

"We call to Grandmother Spider, mother, she who is teacher. She who is devoted to protecting and caring for her young. We call to you, Grandmother Spider to join us as we weave our web in this rite that we may honor you as we honor and celebrate that we are a part of you. Hail and welcome Grandmother Spider."

Cord Magick Exercise
What are you weaving? Are you consciously aware of the threads you are spinning? Of who you are connecting to and with? Are you aware of the web of life that we are all woven together with?

Chant: Weaving Our Way *www.youtube.com/watch?v=V2qmLrbHCtA*
"Weaving our way between the worlds, awakening we touch the source. And when we dream and when we open, we remember who we are."
Chant by Suzanne Sterling from her album "Wings".

Once the chanting is complete, you can begin to cut the cords that bind you all together.

Give thanks to Grandmother Spider – She who weaves the web of life.
Open the medicine wheel – Open the circle.
Hail and Farewell:
North – Earth, Evening, Bear, Winter
West – Water, Dusk, Salmon, Autumn
South – Fire, Heat of Afternoon, Summer, Wolf
East – Sunrise, New Day, Eagle, Springtime

CELEBRATE YOUR RITUAL WITH LIBATIONS OF CAKES AND ALE

She Who Weaves the World: Grandmother Spider – A Native American Goddess

Spider Woman, also known as Na ashje'ii Asdzaa (pronounced: nah-ahsh-jay-ee ahs-dzah) is one of the most important deities honored by the Navajo people. Spider Woman taught weaving, agriculture and is one who restores all things back into balance. She is a 'save the day' kind of goddess. Some honor her in a similar fashion to the Hopi tribe who consider this Spider Woman to be a grandmother and the one who wove the world into existence, she being the one who created humans. The Cherokee believe it was spider that brought light to the people. All these tribes share spider as a benevolent mother who is kind, nurturing and caring deity who acts as a guide, mentor and protector.

In my garden is a wolf spider. These amazing spiders are known for being devoted mothers. The spider in my garden is currently carrying her babies on her back. This is common for wolf spiders, which safe guard their egg sac, carrying it with them everywhere they go until the eggs hatch. Then they carry the babies on their back until they are fully developed, which can take weeks. No wonder we have a deity that is a spider. This act of devotion and love is so powerful it's hard to not look at spiders in an observation mode and not be fascinated and in awe.

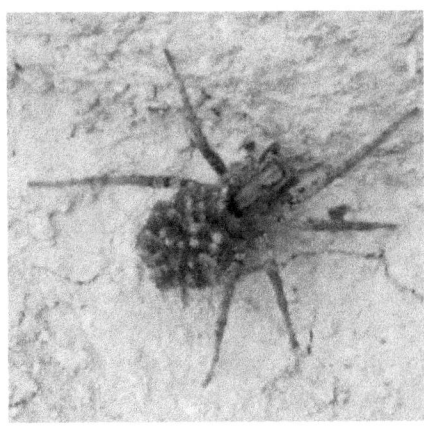

There are many myths and legends about Spider Woman and Grandmother Spider. My most favorite is a children's book called "Grandmother Spider Brings the Sun" by Geri Kearns. It is written by a Navajo woman and tells the story of how Grandmother Spider brought the light of the sun to her people. It is told from the perspective of animals with wolf being the leader and seeking a way to have light in the darkness.

In the book "Grandmother Spider and the Web of Life" by Taino Ti, it is written:

> "When the Universe was still so dark that not even shadows could be seen in the night, Grandmother Spider sat in her web in the Sky World, waiting and watching. No one knows how old Grandmother Spider is, or how long she sat waiting for the Universal Mind to awaken. But, every Creature Being who has ever lived knows her song and dance as the weaver of the Web of Life.
>
> From her web, Grandmother Spider observed the first thoughts as the Universal Mind awakened from the dream. Seven energy beings floated out from the shining light in the center of the Universal Mind and solidified into bright, shining stars who went out to take their places in the Sky World. Grandmother Spider took a very deep breath and softly began to sing her weaving song while she danced across the sky. As she spun her thread, Grandmother Spider envisioned the Web of Life. Within moments, she had woven her web connecting the seven stars and creating the Spirit Doorway through which all of the rest of life would enter.
>
> The seven stars reflected the spectrum of all colors within their glow. Dancing with the colored light, shadows came into being as the darkness took form. More thoughts flowed from the Universal Mind, entered through the Doorway of the Seven Stars, and took their places in the Sky World. These became more stars, suns and planets. Then, many other thoughts entered the Universe, each one taking a specific place according to the universal dream of harmony. Each thought was a spirit essence who dreamed an individual dream for manifesting life. Grandmother Spider spun her web around each new energy being and the Universal Web of Life shimmered in the reflection of Great Mystery's light.
>
> Singing her song and weaving the Web of Life, Grandmother Spider continued with her work. The Sky World filled with light and life as her creative process unfolded. As the stars, suns and planets prepared to give birth to their children, Grandmother Spider spun her cord even

longer, so that all of the newly born could be included in the Web of Life. Grandmother Spider continues to weave the Web of Life throughout every cycle of creation.

All life everywhere in the Universe is connected by the Web of Life. We are not separate beings. We are each a part of the Great Mystery, manifesting as an individual awareness in a separate physical body, but sharing the same energy as all other life. The energy web is anchored within our center and is our connection to the Great Mystery.

Along with Grandmother Spider's web cord, we carry within our center our dream for living that includes a promise and a purpose. Before we came into the Earthwalk, we chose the gifts and talents that help us create the reality that we envisioned. We also chose the lessons and challenges that motivate our learning and growth. Our dream for living carries a specific vibration of sound and color that guides our spirit essence in its flight from the Universal Mind, through the Sacred Cave, and into the womb of our physical mother. During our Earthwalk, we live our choices and lessons, and develop our talents and gifts, as we meet each situation and challenge of our growth. We must remember our purpose and promise and focus our life in this direction if we are to be happy and fulfilled.

Grandmother Spider weaves the Web of Life around us when our spirit essence enters its physical body inside the womb of our mother. From feet to head, our spirit essence is woven together with our physical body as Grandmother Spider sings her weaving song to us. When she completes her weaving, Grandmother Spider does not cut the cord, but leaves an energy trail with her weft thread that goes out from our center to connect with the next Creature Being that will enter the Web of Life.

The gift of Grandmother Spider is the personal energy web that we walk with throughout our entire life. This energy web allows our spirit essence to experience our senses, emotional feelings and physical pains and pleasures. This connection also allows our physical body to develop an intuitive perception of Universal Wisdom. Through the web, we can work with energy for creativity and healing. Our personal energy web maintains our connection to the Web of Life and the Great Mystery. This gift of Grandmother Spider insures that we are never alone, for through it we always share the love of All Our Relations.

Our energy web surrounds our physical body, enveloping it with a vibrating energy that is our personal rhythm. Our energy web is connected to our physical body through energy centers that are the communication channels between our physical body and spirit essence.

Our mind is the link between body and spirit essence, interpreting and directing the flow of energy back and forth. Breathing and movement enables our body to direct energy and our thoughts to affect our physical health. To live in comfort, we need to maintain a balance of body, mind and spirit within our personal energy web.

Grandmother Spider is always busy with her work, as the creation of life is happening at every moment. After connecting each Creature Being within her vibrating threads, Grandmother Spider goes on to the next, spinning out a continuous cord in her never-ending dance. A Creature Being enters the Earthwalk, then a Plant Person, a Stone Person, a Water Person, a Four-Legged, a Two-Legged, and on and on. For each of these, Grandmother Spider weaves a personal energy web and extends her cord out from this Creature's center to continue on with the weaving of the Web of Life.

The Web of Life is a beautiful braid that holds the energy of all life together. Grandmother Spider's dance of spinning and weaving continues indefinitely, as new patterns within the web are being woven every moment when each new life enters the Earthwalk. At the other end of Grandmother Spider's tapestry, the web is always unraveling, as every spirit essence travels back through the doorway of the Sacred Cave to the Spirit World when life is complete.

All life shares an equal place within the Web of Life. The gifts and contributions of each and every Creature Being are very important for the survival of Mother Earth. Each Creature Being, in following through with the performance of their specific life task, affects the welfare of all the other Creature Beings in the web. Without the benefit of even one Creature's work, the Web of Life would lack the energy of wholeness necessary for the circle of life's cycles to continue on with their rhythm."

WEAVE AND SPIN

Weave and spin, weave and spin This is how the work begins Mend and heal, mend and heal Take the dream and make it real On the same wheel we spin Into life and out again One is many, many one Brewing in Her cauldron strand by strand, hand over hand Thread by thread, we weave our web

BY STARHAWK

CHAPTER NINETEEN

COYOTE

MEDICINE AND MAGICK

Coyotes are native to North America. They are smaller in size and stature than their relatives the wolf. Some may be familiar with coyote by their other names of American jackal, prairie wolf or brush wolf. There are nineteen subspecies of coyote.

Coyotes do not have a glorified reputation of honor and respect like their cousin the wolf. Rather, coyotes are seen as tricksters, a nuisance and a bother. Their "attitude" or aggressive behavior with a hint of mischievousness rather links them to the behavior and reputation of foxes.

In size coyotes are much smaller than wolves. Even domesticated dogs of average breed like the golden retriever are larger than coyotes. Like wolves, coyotes have pack mentality and ranking within the pack puts the alpha male in charge of breeding and basically everything within the pack. Coyotes are monogamous and have been known on rare occasions to mate with domesticated dogs, which results in a breed called "coydogs".

The major threat to coyotes is humans. Due to their rapid rate of breeding and the harm they do to livestock, coyotes have been hunted, trapped and killed, oftentimes not even for sport but for population control. Here where I live you can hunt and kill coyotes, send in their ears as proof and receive money in exchange for the service you provided.

In Native myth and legends *coyote* becomes a character; a deity who is "anthropomorphic" (attribution of human traits, emotions, intentions) and takes on the physical characteristics of the canine species coyote. In some of these myths and legends coyote is sacred, divine and holy. In others he is malevolent, mischievous and not one to be trusted.

The Maidu people of California and Central Sierra Nevada believe that in the beginning the first primal being was "Earth Maker" who floated on the waters. Whilst floating, Earth Maker comes to meet coyote and together they sing to birth the world. Afterwards the Earth Maker created people and coyote promised to poison the world with evil. Earth Maker in anger demands that coyote be hunted and destroyed by the people. However, coyote is smart and trick; always outsmarting the hunters. Thus Earth Maker succumbs and gives up the fight acknowledging that coyote has a power that matches his own.

In most of the myths and legends, coyote shares very similar characteristics with raven as both being masters of trickery. Both raven and coyote are scavengers and known for picking the bones clean on carcasses. Both raven and coyote have a somewhat negative reputation counteracted with a very mysterious and enlightened reputation of great esteem. It is easy to define coyote as a guide of self acceptance in that we should all acknowledge that within us are both negative and positive traits. I often think of myself as the "tye-dye sheep of my family," some aspects of my character are well received and some not so much. Just like coyote; there is good and bad, light and dark, trickery and wisdom.

In this chapter we embrace coyote as one who brings balance. One who is both wise and playful and at times a bit obnoxious. Coyote medicine is centered on taking one's self-sabotaging traits and learning to embrace them as part of the whole, rather than something to be rid of or ashamed of.

In his book *"Animal Speak"* Ted Andrews states, "The coyote teaches the balance of wisdom and folly and how they both go hand in hand. The image of the wise fool has been used in the lore of many societies. This is the individual who seems to be a simpleton and yet their words and actions have a much greater wisdom than is initially recognized. Are you not seeing the wisdom of your life and its events?"

COYOTE AS THE FOOL

The deck of Tarot has been around since about the 15th century in Europe. In the late 18th century the Tarot cards started being used as a source of divination. A Tarot deck consists of 78 cards, 22 are the Major Arcana cards and 56 are the Minor Arcana cards. For the purpose of this book we will focus on the Major Arcana cards. For quick and simple reference visit the biddytarot.com website or read "Tarot for One" by Courtney Weber.

The Major Arcana cards (also called trump cards) represent life lessons, karmic influences, archetypal themes that are currently influencing your life. These cards represent the structure of human consciousness and hold the keys to life lessons passed down through the ages. The very first card in the Tarot deck and Major Arcana is The Fool – he is the main character, the star. The deck of Tarot tells the story of The Fool who, along his life travels, meets new teachers, learns new lessons and at the end of his journey he conquers the world. This is known as The Fool's Journey. Diving into the journey of The Fool is one of the most helpful ways of learning the art of reading the Tarot. The Fool card is the most powerful card in the entire deck.

The Tarot deck is useful for in-depth questions that require in-depth answers. Each card in the Major Arcana represents someone that you the reader either is, has met or will need to assist you in life's journey. The Fool is both the beginning and the end. Typically the traditional Fool card in the most common deck the "Rider-Waite" shows a young man standing on the edge of a cliff, his gaze upwards, not a care in the world; he carries a small knapsack, holds a white rose in his left hand and has a happy pup at his feet. The Fool is unique to himself, a character all on his own. In the deck, this card is numbered 0, he is a wild card.

In Norse mythology we understand that Loki, though not a god but a giant, is honored in similar fashion as The Fool card. He stands alone, authentic, wild and, depending on how you play the game of life, The Fool and Loki can be a welcome sight or an unknown character pulled to take you off course or to show you a new direction. Either way, Loki and The Fool are both tricksters that keep you alert and on your toes. Much like coyote.

In myths and legends of the Navajo people, coyote is a pivotal player in one's game of life. Coyote is both good and bad. He is unpredictable and a bringer of order all at the same time. Coyote pushes the boundaries and limits, all the while encouraging growth and the bravery to step into the unknown or rather step towards the cliff of unknown like The Fool card.

Many modern Tarot decks have embraced coyote as The Fool, such as the "Animal Wisdom Tarot" by Dawn Brunke and the "Native American Tarot" by Magda Weck Gonzalez, to name two of many decks with coyote featured as the star.

Coyote and the traditional Fool, along with Loki from the Norse, all represent wit, curiosity, free spirited, taking risks, being clever, spontaneous, light hearted, playful and moving forward without a care in the world. Coyote is a mirror as The Fool of all the possibilities that we can embrace if we would just take a chance.

Coyote is the poster child for one who can laugh at oneself and still keep going. Think of the wisest person you know, they probably have the best sense of humor. Whenever I pull The Fool card in my readings, I always welcome coyote energy as a reminder to lighten up a bit, take a chance, put your best foot or paw forward and just keep going. Trust the natural flow of karma and just go for it.

COYOTE AS THE TRICKSTER

In mythology, the trickster is an archetypal character; a key figure that shows an immense amount of wit, intellect and plays tricks or games that encourage those around him to break the rules of conventional behavior and step into the unknown. By definition; trickster means a person who cheats or deceives people. I have always pondered whether people are actually tricked or are they tested to think beyond the norm, questioning their own intellect which ultimately sends them into a spiral of challenges that really were all based upon their own decision to believe or not believe the one who did the tricking.

Loki in Norse mythology is mentioned in almost every myth and legend. Why? He is easily bored and enjoys challenging the gods out of their normal day to day godness and introduces something uncomfortable or enticing. Either way, through his taunts, the gods are always given a choice to react. Just like coyote energy, medicine and magick. If, through your observations and seeing the signs and symbols you begin to see, hear or notice more coyotes than before, chances are you are being sent the trickster as a form of a challenge to break out of the mundane and embrace the realm of unknown possibilities.

In our lives one thing is certain; trials, challenges, obstacles will always pop up. Some experience these more than others but there is no denying that they happen and will continue to happen. Coyote as trickster is simply encouraging a new outlook, watch your reactions and play the game or journey of life with a bit of pizzazz and brassy boldness.

The only thing we ever have absolute control over is our reactions to these trials, challenges and obstacles. To the Native Americans, coyote was the ultimate teacher. To the Hopi people coyote taught the people through his antics and adventures. Giving them a sense of moral insight and a lesson in disobedience. To the Hopi and Lakota Sioux people, he was not honored, rather looked at as an example of what not to do.

The Cherokee coyote was loyal, adaptable and, as trickster, taught humor in uncomfortable situations. He was the bringer of new beginnings and endings. To the Navajo people, coyote brought about the stars. He also was one that was an omen of misfortune or rather insight. If coyote crossed your path, it was a message something was coming.

There are so many different stories, myths and legends with coyote as key figure. These stories of coyote as trickster have been told for centuries around the fire as a way of teaching the people, by coyote being the example. Coyote has interactions with so many different animals on his journey through life that he is a pivotal character of both the good and the bad. To quote the movie *Brave*, "Legends are lessons, they ring with truths."

To make the most of Coyote medicine is to honor the coyote essence within yourself. To see your faults and accomplishments as all part of the journey. To laugh at oneself instead of embracing self sabotage. If you have ever heard a pack of coyotes howling and barking; they sound like they are laughing. Maybe they are laughing at us. Maybe they are the master teachers who we have underestimated and overlooked.

"A fool thinks himself to be wise, but a wise

man knows himself to be a fool."

WILLIAM SHAKESPEARE

ACTIVATION CONNECTION THROUGH MEDITATION

Allow yourself an interruption-free space where you can settle into a comfortable position. Here in this space, take your focus and awareness to your breath. Inhale to the count of four and exhale to the count of four. Repeat this breath pattern for about three to six minutes or until you can physically feel your entire body relax. Consciously check in with each part of your physical body from your head all the way down to your feet. Relaxing and releasing tension with each exhale.

Here in this state of calm, close your eyes and mentally clear it of distracting thoughts, breathe out the 'to do' lists and the worries. Allow your mind to enter a realm of stillness. Tapping into your intuitive mind, your source of imagination, see yourself in the desert. Feel the sand beneath your feet; it is warmed from the sun. Observe your surroundings, the red rocks, cactuses and desert brush surround you. Off in the distance you hear barking, yipping and some howling.

Coyotes are singing. They may be unaware of your presence or they don't seem to care as their song continues. Hear them, feel that energy of their song getting louder and louder! Breathe that in. Breathe in the ability to laugh, to just be and not care who is around.

Allow yourself to absorb coyote medicine. Allow yourself to stretch, to move and to become one with coyote. Feel how light hearted and whimsical your body becomes as you call upon coyote. Coyote is all about the heat of the sun, he is a fire dancer! Coyote is brave and whole unto self. Coyote doesn't answer to anyone. Embody that! Feel that confidence seep into every pore of your body.

EMBODYING COYOTE THROUGH MOVEMENT – TRANCE DANCING

Yoga is a peaceful and challenging movement of muscles and bones designed to heal and create inner peace within the body and mind. Coyote doesn't want you to embrace inner peace but rather move into a place of acceptance through the movement of dancing.

After you have completed the activation meditation, take all that channeled confidence onto the dance floor. This can be your kitchen, your bedroom, outdoors while you are hiking or maybe you are fortunate enough to have a bonfire. Either way, no matter what your surroundings are, embrace coyote through dance.

Everyone can dance! There are no steps to learn. Just move! Turn on your favorite music or even better turn on some shamanic trance drumming, Danheim, Wardruna or other Viking inspired music and begin.

When moving into a trance state of shapeshifting, it is a good idea to have a designated spot and specific time frame when first trance dancing. Begin with three songs. Have them ready to play. With the first song start with your eyes closed, visualize a fire if you don't have one and let the beat of the drums move through you as you.

Move your body in any way that feels right for you. Coyote doesn't wait for permission or instructions. Coyote feels! Coyote does! Breathe in coyote and move, dance in a form of celebration because you simply can!

"Life is the dancer and you are the dance."

EKHART TOLLE

"ODE TO LOKI – GOD OF SHAPESHIFTING"

Hail the God of shapeshifting. Loki of the Norse mythology is one of duality. Some people love him and some people loathe him. He is the trickster and he is coyote medicine and magick. Loki, like coyote, is often not invited to the feast. Rather, to say his name is to invite and welcome in chaos.

A dear friend of mine described Loki as one who enters the realms through the cracks of chaos. As shapeshifter, Loki is the master. In almost all of the myths and legends, Loki has the ability to shift physical form into non human forms in order to obtain knowledge and ways of taking down the gods.

He is the ultimate challenger and breaker of the normative. Loki is the God of Trickery. A son of the Giant Farbauti and later a blood brother through oath making with the All Father Odin. Loki became known as one of the Aesir Gods. Loki is a pivotal character and figure. He takes center stage.

His mischievousness and erratic behavior captivates most but can repel some. He was neither a fan nor enemy of the gods. Loki just did what he was good at and that's to shake things up! He tested the boundaries and challenged everyone with wit. He was not a warrior, didn't have a physical weapon. Instead, his mind was his greatest tool.

It is Loki that gave the God's of the Aesir some of their most prized possessions. From Odin's spear, Thor's hammer to the eight legged horse "Sleipnir" that Odin rode, Loki was responsible. Yet he is oftentimes spoken of in secret and disdain.

Loki is a magician and master at shifting into anything from the tiniest flea, to hawk, to other people. Loki has no limitations! He isn't bound by rules. He is a breaker of them and thus he was given the nasty title as Oath Breaker. Even in my small community there are heathen groups who do not honor Loki or dare to mention his name.

Some folks even liken Loki to Lucifer as Loki's name means "light bringer" and Lucifer is the "shining one." Both have been cast out and given negative connotations. Loki, coyote and Lucifer are all esteemed at creating chaos. Through chaos we are forced to adapt, change perspective, get back up and try again. All three are catalysts of change. Loki, like coyote, is a mover and shaker. Lucifer offered an apple in the Garden of Eden in the guise of a serpent. Lucifer is a shapeshifter as well. The apple or rather "forbidden fruit" represented knowledge of good and evil.

Loki has many titles from God of Chaos, Mischief, Trickster, Father of Wolves, Firestarter to Mother of Sleipnir. Loki, like coyote, has so much to offer if you just embrace the chaos of life. It is Loki's monstrous children that bring about the much dreaded and feared "Ragnarok" or rather end of the gods' reign as was known at the time.

Was Ragnarok really something that was feared or rather something that was looked at as inevitable? After all everything ends...Everyone dies. Some believe that Ragnarok was embraced; a lesson of how to live with honor, dignity, courage and to ultimately face fate. We have Loki to thank for all of that! Just like we have coyote to thank. If it wasn't for coyote and Loki's mishaps and adventures, we wouldn't have the courage to venture out and explore all possibilities. We wouldn't have boundaries to push against, challenge us and to overcome.

To embrace Loki is to honor The Fool, dance like coyote and step out to the edge of the cliff of what could be and take a risk.

EMBRACING COYOTE THROUGH RITUAL ACTIVATION

The intent with this ritual activation is to call upon coyote as a mirror to encourage acceptance of chaos. To embrace some form of chaos magic and call upon whatever ideas, practices that one feels in the here and now.

Disconnecting from any previous dogma or ritual definition. Rather, doing what feels good in the moment. Chaos magick is all about being out of the box and breaking free from paradigms or conformities.

This ritual can be as simple or complex as you want it to be. To help you break free from patterns, how to's and outlines; simply clear your mind and space. Ask yourself what is next? If you decide to set up an altar, what does that look like to you? Do you need an altar? Do you need sacred tools as defined by other practices? Do you need to sit down and formulate an intention or can you just enter the present moment of unknowns, let go and experience?

"Chaos magic is an attitude, a philosophy that promotes experimentation, play, and creativity while discarding dogmatic rules. Chaos magic points out that the techniques more than the symbols are what matter and that our belief in a system is actually what makes it work."

ANDREIH VITIMUS

Create a space for you. Make it spontaneous and just allow yourself to feel what's next. You can take yourself back through the connection meditation and trance dancing to help you step into the realm of the unknown and fully embody coyote medicine. Or you can just sit and chat with Loki about the possibilities of what's out there not being really known or open for pre-interpretation. Either way, take some time to honor coyote, or Loki, as both mirrors and trail blazers.

Journal your chaos ritual experience.

WAYS OF LIVING AS COYOTE

To fully embody coyote is to allow and step away from the need to always be in control. To release and let go of the heaviness of 'to do' lists and be more spontaneous, light hearted and be willing to take some risks.

1. Laugh more! Laugh at yourself more! If you need a nudge in this area then do jumping jacks naked. It is amazingly funny how your body jiggles and moves when doing jumping jacks. This simple act of being

able to laugh at yourself can be incredibly healing.

2. Step out of your comfort zone, do something that you wouldn't normally do. Try something new. Maybe a different way of dressing, eat something different, go somewhere you have never been. Branch out and gift yourself with new experiences.

3. Dance! Wildly! Remember that "Friends" episode where Rachel and Phoebe went running and they both looked like crazy fools? Do something a bit crazy! Dance like no one is watching!

4. Stop caring what people think! This is your life and your life experience. So who cares what others think? You are never going to please everyone, so stop trying and please yourself.

5. Be bold, be true, be you! In all things! Own your authenticity!

"All great changes are preceded by chaos"

DEEPAK CHOPRA

CONTINUING THE PATH OF THE SHAPESHIFTER

Looking to animals as guides, messengers and teachers is not a new practice. It is not "new age" or metaphysical. It is vital! Animals have survived in the harshest of climates, amongst the most notorious predators and are thriving. However, there is one predator that has done the most damage and continues to be the number one threat to ALL, and that is us. Humans are the greatest predators.

Human beings' desire to own, conquer and exhibit dominion over not just the animals but over the earth herself will very likely be the downfall of humanity. Unless we begin to create a shift right now as a collective pack, clan, tribe, colony and civilization.

We are the deadliest of all predators and we are attacking our very livelihood through ignorance, ego and the power-seeking need to dominate.

When and how will we learn? When will we step up and be the change? Most importantly; is it too late? Have we done irreparable damage? Can we stop the madness and look to the animals as our ancestors once did?

Don't we have a responsibility to the future generation to teach by example love, honor and respect for all things. Children are sponges! They come into this existence hungry and ready to learn, it is part of their very survival. If we were to show children how to care for the earth and the animals, things could shift back into a balanced state. But the time is now!

What if we stopped killing animals and hanging their carcasses on our walls as trophies? As shifters of shapes, we can do more than just energetically connect with the attributes of animals through meditation. We can act through example of how to live on this earth that we all share. We can embody their essence in all things.

We can call upon swan energy when things become stressful and remember to float. We can step into the strength and poise of horse and stand up for what we know to be our truths. We can take care of each other as if we all belong to the same wolf pack or lion pride. We can rise above our need to react and call upon raven and hawk for a new perspective. By peeling off the layers of armor that we hide behind out of fear or ego we can expose the deep richness of our authenticity like scorpion; we also know that we can put that armor on if and when we need to in order to feel protected. We can become environmentally in honor of bee and become aware of just how much we need this earth and rely upon it. We can grow a garden for our colony. We can step down off the pedestal of pride and ownership and become stewards of the land. We can be docile, yet powerful like cow and mother ourselves back to a balanced and healthy state of being. We can look to cobra and know there is a time to strike, spit venom and protect our own. We can embody spider and create, embrace artistic expression and weave together stronger relationships with those who we call family. We can move in celebration of our bodies and dive deep into the chaos like coyote to create inevitable change within as without.

Every day we are downloading information, given signs or symbols, keys, wisdom from the grave, the beyond, the other realms, but are we listening? Are we seeing? Are we doing?

Currently we are seeing a rise in people embracing witchcraft, Wicca and what is considered New Age practices. Yet most have missed the very point and definition of responsibility that those who practice the Craft are embodying and that is stewardship to the land. Witches are healers, wise one's that work hand in hand with Nature as constant students. It is a humbling role and it should be.

Yet we see the opposite. We see people owning the title of witch and practicing witchcraft like it's the trendy, cool thing to do. Yet there is very little follow through and very little witchcraft being practiced. People are "reclaiming" the word witch. But was it ever a title that one would want to "reclaim?" In the burning times, to be called a witch was to be given a death sentence, it was a dirty word. How about we "claim" the title witch, make it our own but actually practice witchcraft?

The ancient civilizations knew something that we as modern humans have forgotten and that is pack mentality. Embracing agricultural living isn't just working hand in hand with nature to grow food and raise livestock but to care for each other in one's community. How many modern day "witches" do you see doing that? How many of the self proclaimed witches do you see kneeling at the feet of their grandmothers and listening to their wisdom? How many do you see kneel at the roots of the great oak trees and talk to them, listen to them and be with them? 'Self proclaimed' is simply one person deciding to own a title and most adopt things that are depicted in the media and by Hollywood on how to implement their practice. Yet, there is so much more!

Let's go back to the basics. Let's look to the ancient ones, the old ones and really honor the mentorship and guidance that the "old gods", plants and animals have to offer us still today in our modern, technology-driven world. There is a reason that the ancient civilizations considered gods and animals interchangeable and there is a reason why almost every god or goddess from just about every pantheon is linked with a specific animal.

If people today were to look at animals as godlike beings, they would be given more respect. Not to mention better homes and living conditions. We can shift this beautiful planet but it will take drastic change from the collective pack or pride. We need to stop embracing division and work together for the greater good. If we can't do that, then what will the future generation have? We can teach by example and come together.

We can start living more consciously aware of what we eat, where our meat comes from, how it is gathered and how we prepare it. Imagine if everyone practiced real kitchen witchery and made each meal a ritual. Imagine thanking the animal that gave its life, most likely unwillingly, for one's consumption. How would that change the way you lived?

As witches, we can be the movers and the shakers, the change makers, but we need to become activists and start protecting our mother, this amazing planet that we all live on. We can begin to see each other as divine, sentient and godlike. After all, we are animals too! If we honor each other and allow each other to vibrate in our own animal, instinctual manner then we can begin to live more consciously aware and begin to practice some real witchcraft.

Let's call upon the old gods as examples and learn from their myths and legends. Let's once again see their energy, their essence and their attributes in the animals around us and in each other.

Let's teach the young ones how to care for, love, honor and look to Nature for guidance. Maybe they can undo the neglect that we have chosen in our effort to discover more advanced technology and mainstream our lives into the social media world. After all, "children are the future."